Str

Somers Town and the Railway Lands

ISBN 0 9044491 54 4

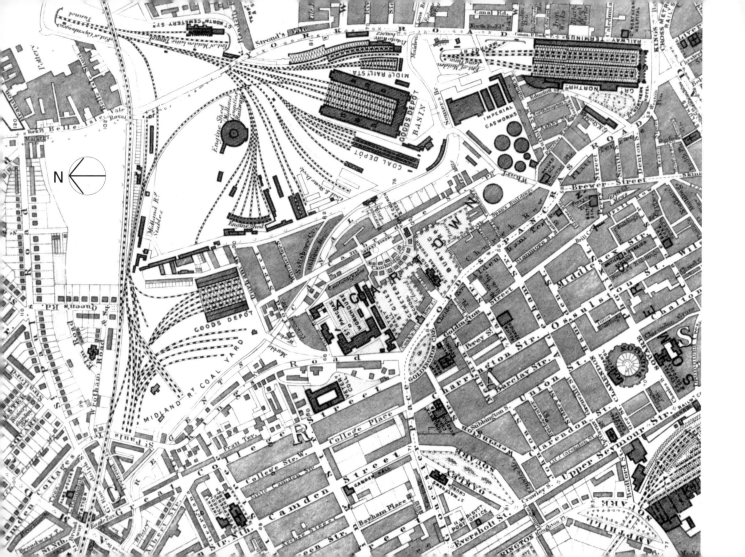

This map (Stanford, 1863) shows Somers Town, Agar Town and the Railway Lands of the Great Northern Railway. York Road (now York Way) is to the east and runs alongside the factories of Belle Isle. The Midland Railway has made its first incursion into the area with its coal yard in northern Agar Town – Elm Lodge (William Agar's house) is already encircled by railway lines – but work has not yet started either on its main London approach route through Agar Town (along the line of Queen's Road in the north) nor on its terminal (on the site of Perry, Smith and Denton Streets, in the south). Note the prominent circular building of the Polygon in Clarendon Square.

Streets of St Pancras

Somers Town
and the Railway Lands

A survey of streets, buildings and former residents in a part of Camden

Compiled by   Camden History Society

Edited by   Steven Denford and F Peter Woodford

Designed by   Ivor Kamlish

Diagram of the walks
(for detailed street map
see back cover)

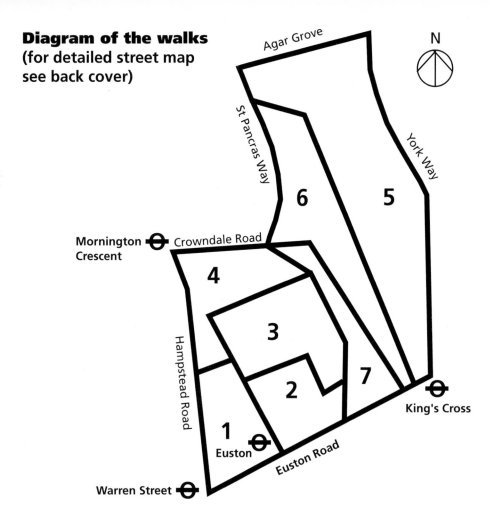

Agar Grove

N

St Pancras Way

York Way

6

5

Mornington Crescent

Crowndale Road

4

3

2

7

Hampstead Road

1

Euston

Euston Road

King's Cross

Warren Street

Contents

Street names in this book and their origins

Later 20th-century names of no known historical relevance are omitted.

* (sometime) property of the Russell family, Dukes of Bedford
† no known specific local connection.

Agar
William, C18-C19 lawyer & landowner
Aldenham
Herts. birthplace of Richard Platt
Allensbury
Eastern part of St Pancras Prebendal Manor
Barker
Tom, Mayor of St Pancras 1958-9 (d1970)
Barnby
Sir Joseph, C19 musician †
Battle Bridge
Locality known since 1820s as King's Cross
Blakeney
On Norfolk coast, its salt marshes coincidentally drained by an Agar Creek
Bridgeway
Variant on earlier [Lord] Bridgewater †
Brill
The Brill, farm & farmhouse
Camley
Variant on earlier Cambridge †
Cardington
Village near Bedford*
Chalton
English village, significance unknown †
Charles
Charles Fitzroy, Lord Southampton
Charrington
Brewing company; street lay on Brewers' estate

Chenies
Former Bucks. property of Duke of Bedford
Christopher
?Christopher Kite, local sanitary & heating engineer
Churchway
Ancient footpath to old parish church
Clarendon
Clarendon Square (after Earl of †) once adjoined
Cobourg
Leopold of Saxe-Coburg married Princess Charlotte† in 1816
Coopers
?From Coopers' Arms, former local pub
Crace
J G Crace, interior decorator of St Pancras New Church
Cranleigh
Cranleigh† Houses, flats built in 1934
Crowndale
Farm near Tavistock, Devon *
Doric
Recalls Euston Station's lost Doric 'arch'
Drummond
Lady Caroline, great-granddaughter of 2nd Duke of Grafton
Elm Friars
Another name for Allensbury (q.v.)

Euston
Suffolk seat of Dukes of Grafton
Eversholt
Village near Woburn Abbey *
Exmouth
Admiral Lord, hero of Napoleonic wars †
Foundry
Wailes' iron foundry was nearby
George
Probably George, 2nd Baron Southampton
Goldington
Village near Bedford *
Goods
Led to GNR goods yard
Gower
Earl of, father-in-law of 4th Duke of Bedford
Grafton
Duke of, local landowner
Granary
Bass Ale Stores, *aka* 'The Granary' were adjacent
Hampden
?From John, C17 Parliamentarian
Harrington
Earl of, father-in-law of 7th Duke of Bedford
Hurdwick
Another farm near Tavistock *
Lancing
Sussex seaside town †

Lidlington
Village near Ampthill, Beds.*
Maiden
'Midden' (refuse heap); *or* image of Virgin
Medburn
Farm at Aldenham (*q.v.*)
Melton
Place name; derivation unknown †
Midland
Midland Railway terminus adjoins
Millbrook
Another village near Ampthill *
Neville
Miss Edith, SPHA activist
Oakley
Another village near Bedford*
Ossulston
A 'hundred' of Middlesex †
Penryn
Welsh place name †
Phoenix
Possibly an obscure (c1800) tavern
Platt
Richard, C16 brewer & landowner
Polygon
The Polygon, late-C18 'experimental building'
Purchese
Frederick, C19 St Pancras churchwarden
Regnart
Family members were presidents of Maple's

(St) Pancras
Patron saint of children, martyred 304 AD
St Paul's
Local ecclesiatical parish
Starcross
Devon village on the Exe estuary
Stephenson
Robert, L&NW Railway engineer
Tolmers
One (defunct) source of the New River
Weir
Probably Alexander, local publican
Wellesley
Arthur, Duke of Wellington †
Werrington
Village near Peterborough *
Wrotham
Kentish village †
York
London & York Railway

Historical overview

The parish of St Pancras, Middlesex, once stretched for some four miles, north to south, from Highgate Village to the borders of Holborn and St Giles. The fraction of its area covered in this book embraces the parish's historic heartland.

Occupying a knoll beside the River Fleet, St Pancras Old Church (in Pancras Road) was probably built as early as the 4th century, on a previously pagan site. It is thought to have been rebuilt and dedicated to St Pancras at the time of St Augustine's mission to England in 597 AD. Pancratius was a 14-year-old Roman, martyred in 304, who became the patron saint of the young, and avenger of false oaths and perjury (for example, William the Conqueror made Harold swear by St Pancratius).

A small settlement grew up around the church. The parish was recorded in Domesday as 'Pancras', by which name the locality was long popularly known. By the 14th century, and maybe forced by the constant flooding of the River Fleet to seek drier ground, the villagers had migrated north to the area now known as Kentish Town. A chapel-of-ease was erected there; the old mother church became neglected, and was long used only for weddings and funerals.

Our survey area remained sparsely populated until the later 18th century, as open country with a few scattered houses and wayside taverns. Dairy farms supplied milk for the metropolis, and hay was grown for the capital's horses. Londoners used the area as a rural retreat, enjoying its country lanes, frequenting its tea gardens, or taking the waters at Pancras Wells beside the Fleet. There were few roads, mostly running south to north: the ancient road to Hampstead (now Hampstead Road); Gray's Inn Lane (now Pancras Road and St Pancras Way); and Maiden Lane (York Way). Fig Lane (Crowndale Road) provided the only east–west link. Haunted by highwaymen, the roads were regarded as dangerous, especially after dark.

Presaging change was the advent of the New Road from Paddington to Islington, the Camden section of which has been known since 1857 as Euston Road. Authorised by an Act of Parliament, it was constructed in 1756 and maintained by two Turnpike Trusts.

As London expanded, many local fields were given over to the making of bricks, supplied both to local builders and to a wider market. Dust heaps arose for the disposal of the capital's waste; a smallpox hospital was opened at Battle Bridge in 1793–4; and two West End parishes (St Giles-in-the-Fields and St James', Piccadilly) established overspill burial grounds in the district, each later converted by St Pancras Vestry into public gardens.

Beginning with ribbon development along the New Road around 1780, our area was gradually built up, as landowners leased land to speculative house builders in the hope of maximising their incomes. (See 'A note on land ownership', p 11.) Development was slow and fitful, held back by successive slumps in the building trade.

In 1783, Lord Somers leased his Brill Farm estate for house building, the first phase of which was completed in the next decade. 'Somers Town', when first built, was indeed a self-contained new 'town', separated from London by acres of open fields. It was intended as a respectable suburb, but the leases granted by the noble lord gave him little influence over what was erected. Although early houses had generous gardens, many of these were soon built over with poor-quality housing.

In later housing developments, from 1830 onwards, landlords sought to learn from this mistake, attempting to exercise more control over what was built. West of Somers Town, in one corner of Lord Southampton's estate, Euston Square and its environs were built, mostly in the early 19th century, as a northward extension of Bloomsbury, and with first-rate houses surrounding the square itself. To the north, the Duke of Bedford developed his Fig's Mead estate primarily as a middle-class suburb, whose street pattern was deliberately designed to minimise contact with neighbouring Somers Town. The building of 'Bedford New Town', and the development of the Brewers' estate immediately to the east of it, were finally completed only around 1860.

By that time, much of the district had been transformed yet again in the 'transport revolution' of the 19th century. The Regent's Canal, opened to traffic in 1820, passed through our area *en route* from Paddington to the Thames at Limehouse; wharves and warehouses were established along its banks. The canal's importance was soon eclipsed by the advent of the railways, three of which built their termini in close proximity along the

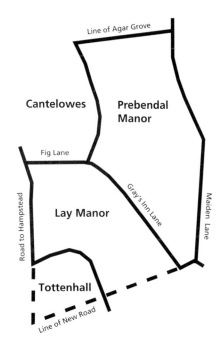

Medieval manors in St Pancras

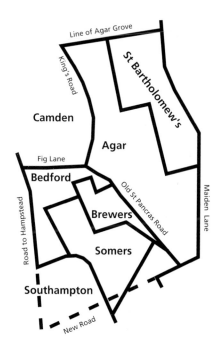

18th-Century estates in the same area

Euston Road. London's first main line, the London & Birmingham (later London & North Western), opened its 'Euston Square' (Euston) station in 1837. Some 15 years later the Great Northern Railway (GNR) established its terminus at King's Cross. The Midland Railway (MR), having initially shared King's Cross, eventually gained a station of its own, next door at 'St

Pancras', in 1868. Determined to outshine its neighbouring rivals, it fronted the station with its magnificent, neo-Gothic, Midland Grand Hotel. The approach lines of the MR's 'London Extension' not only cut controversially through the old parish churchyard, but also led to the destruction of much of Somers Town and the virtual extinction of the short-lived (and much defamed) Agar Town. A vast tract of land on the eastern side of our area was progressively given over to railway use, with numerous goods and coal depots, engine sheds, and many acres of sidings.

Other landmarks in the area's transport history were the construction beneath the Euston Road of the Metropolitan Railway, the world's first underground line, opened in 1863; and the arrival of the local tramway network, opened in 1872 by the London Street Tramways Co., originally horse-powered, electrified in 1909, and replaced by trolleybuses shortly before WW II.

The district's excellent transport links attracted industry: a major gas-works bordered the Regent's Canal, while lighter industries thrived in the area's many yards and mews. The presence of industry, and the smoke and noise from the railways, ensured that the area would never be fashionable. No provision had been made to house the people displaced by the building of the railways, who could only pour into already overcrowded areas nearby. Somers Town evolved into one of London's most notorious slums.

In 1889 St Pancras, previously governed by the parish Vestry, became a Metropolitan Borough, later renowned for its left-wing politics, and eventually absorbed, in 1965, into the new Borough of Camden.

The 20th century saw major change in Somers Town, first through slum clearance. Bug-infested houses were replaced by innovative blocks of flats, some municipal, others erected by the St Pancras House Improvement Society, founded in 1924, and later renamed the St Pancras Housing Association (SPHA; now the St Pancras & Humanist Housing Association). We cannot here do justice to the work of that remarkable body, for the full story of which the reader is referred to Malcolm Holmes' book, *Housing is Not Enough*.

During WW II, the local railway infrastructure was a prime target for enemy bombers, and neighbouring residential streets were also hit. After the war, damaged and blighted housing was replaced by further blocks of council (and SPHA) flats. Some original houses nonetheless survived, to benefit from rehabilitation or 'gentrification' later in the century. Others have been put to corporate use: the many national charities and trade unions which have long had their headquarters in the district have recently been joined by media and information technology firms. Large office blocks dominate the Euston Road, joined latterly by the new British Library, on the site of a former railway depot.

The local residential population has always been very mixed. Early Somers Town attracted many people of a radical persuasion, including atheists, republicans and Chartists. Ever cosmopolitan, the area has found favour with many immigrants from overseas. Somers Town was colonised first by aristocratic and other French émigrés, and later by Spanish refugees. There has always been a significant Irish presence locally since the arrival of the navvies to dig the canal. More recently, since the early 1970s, our area has seen an influx of Bangladeshis and others from the Indian subcontinent.

In the Railway Lands to the north, the demise of wagon-load freight, the collapse of the household coal trade, and the end of steam traction, left an expanse of post-industrial wasteland whose long-term future remains uncertain. In 2002, works for the Channel Tunnel Rail Link are well under way, as much of our area submits to yet another bout of railway-induced upheaval.

A note on land ownership

O F THE MEDIEVAL MANORS (diagram on p 9) underlying our area, two were 'prebends' of St Paul's Cathedral. Property here was granted by the Dean and Chapter to a 'prebendary', who in turn would lease land to a third party under an arrangement known as 'copyhold', so called because each party to the agreement kept a written copy.

Attached to the old parish church was **St Pancras Prebendal Manor**. A survey in 1649 described the prebend farm of Pancras as 75 acres of pastureland, lying between Battle Bridge (King's Cross) and what is now Agar Grove. Three further fields, abutting Maiden Lane (York Way), were held by St Bartholomew's Hospital. That area, known as Allensbury, later evolved into the 'Railway Lands', which we explore in Route 5. The manor house is believed to have stood in the northwest corner of the manor, east of the King's Road (St Pancras Way). There the lawyer William **Agar** bought 70 acres in 1810, erecting for himself a fine mansion called Elm Lodge. His widow, in 1840, leased plots of land to working men for the building of the long-vanished and notorious Agar Town, whose old territory we visit in Route 6.

Further west (and mostly outside our survey area) lay the prebendal manor of **Tottenhall**, a large manor extending from 'Fitzrovia' to Highgate. Its manor house was at 'Tottenham Court', near modern Tolmers Square. Leased by the Crown, likewise appropriated by Parliament, and reclaimed at the Restoration, it had to be sold because of Charles II's extravagances. Acquired by the Earl of Arlington, the copyhold was inherited (together with property at Euston in Suffolk) by his daughter, Isabella. She married Henry Fitzroy, the 9-year-old illegitimate son of Charles II, who became Earl of Euston and 1st Duke of Grafton. In 1780, the soldier Charles Fitzroy, younger brother of the influential 3rd Duke, became Baron **Southampton**. In 1767 he had succeeded in purchasing the freehold of 255 acres of manorial demesne land at a bargain price of £300 per annum, paving the way for the later development of the area around Euston Square (Routes 1 & 2).

Extending southward from Fig Lane, and eventually bisected by the New Road, was a fourth area, known conventionally as the **Lay Manor** of St Pancras. There is some doubt as to whether it ever really existed as such; no manor house has been identified. The so-called manor was once owned by the London Charterhouse. After the Dissolution, land ownership here became very fragmented. Two estates were bequeathed by benevolent Tudors for the benefit of public schools, and were vested in City livery companies as trustees. The **Brewers'** Company managed land west of what is now Pancras Road, given in 1575 by a brewer, Richard Platt, to endow a school at Aldenham (Herts.). Bequeathed three years earlier, and clipping the southeast corner of our territory, was the **Skinners'** Sandhills estate, given by Sir Andrew Judd to benefit Tonbridge School in Kent. Two further estates were owned by peers of the realm. Brill Farm was bought in 1628 by Charles Cocks of the Middle Temple, whose grandson (also Charles) became Baron **Somers** of Evesham, and on whose land was built Somers Town (Routes 2 & 3). Immediately to the north was Fig's Mead, owned by the Russell family (Dukes of **Bedford**), better known as the landlords of nearby Bloomsbury, and who here developed 'Bedford New Town' (Route 4).

Most of the landowners mentioned above – or people and places connected with them – are commemorated in the names of streets and buildings we shall encounter on our walks.

Vanished streets of St Pancras

Lost to the Railways
or associated works

London & North Western
Euston Station & approaches:
    Duke Street (off Seymour St)
    Wriothesley Street (p 63)
Hotel (p 20): Seymour Crescent
Carriage sheds (p 19):
    Birchmore Terrace
Westward station extension (p 19):
    Cardington Street (part)
    Whittlebury Street
Demolition by LMS (p 29):
    Euston Crescent

Great Northern Railway
King's Cross Station (p 80):
    Adden Place
    Congreve Street
    Essex Street
    Lower Edmund Street
    Stephenson Street
    Union Place
    Upper Union Place
Adjacent stabling (p 76):
    Back Walk
    Clarence Place

    Pancras Place
    Paradise Row
    Red Lion Place
    Weller's Place
Suburban Station (p 77):
    Ashby Street
    Norfolk Street
    Northampton Street
    Suffolk Street
    Upper Edmund Street

Midland Railway
Line of route (p 86)
    Queen's Road
Line of route and Agar
Town Goods Depot (p 93):
    Bolton Street
    Chichester Street East
    Durham Street
    Durham Terrace
    Kingston Street
    Oxford Street
    Salisbury Street
    Winchester Street
    Winchester Terrace
Line of route, Bass Ale Stores (p 93),
Cambridge Street coal drops (p 90):
    Cambridge Crescent
    Cambridge Row
    Canterbury Place
    Oxford Row
    Oxford Terrace
    York Place

Pancras Road coal drops (p 102):
    Church Hill
    Church Place
    Church Terrace
    Dorset Place
    Essex Place
    King's Place
    Spann's Buildings
    Thornley Place
St Pancras Station & hotel (pp 88 & 104):
    Denton Street
    Egremont Place
    Hertford Street
    Judd Place East
    Perry Street
    Skinners Place
    Smith Street
    Weston Street
Pancras Road realignment (p 88):
    Weston Place
Midland Road (p 102):
    Brewer Street
    Skinner Street
Somers Town Goods Depot (p 44):
    (Site of British Library piazza)
    James Street
    Judd Place West
    West Street
    (South of Chapel Street)
    Beale's Place
    Brill Place
    Caroline Place
    Cottage Place
    Isaacs Place
    John's Place

Marson Street
North Place
Northam's Square
Phillips Buildings
Spann's Place
Stevens Place
Chapel Street itself
(North of Chapel Street)
Brill Crescent
Brill Row
Denton's Buildings
Middlesex Place
Middlesex Street (S)
Old Romney Place
Phoenix Place
Purchese St & Coal Depot (p 46):
Goldington (*late* Brill) Street
Middlesex Street (N)
Stanmore Street
Watford Street

British Rail

New Euston Station (p 29):
Drummond Street (part)
Euston Place
Euston Mews
Euston Street (part)
Melton Mews

Channel Tunnel Rail Link (p 78):
Cheney Road
Clarence Passage
Stanley Passage
Weller's Court

Lost to slum clearance
or residential redevelopment

Hampden House (p 50):
Harris's Place
Parker's Place
Churchway Estate (p 34):
Elizabeth Place
Latham's Court
Seymour Court
York Buildings
Ossulston Estate (pp 41 & 44):
(Site of Levita House)
Chapel Grove
Wilsted Cottages
(Site of Hadstock House)
Eastnor Place
(Site of Chamberlain House)
Tucker's Rents
York Place
(Site of Walker House)
Equity Buildings
Eversholt Estate (p 53):
Clarendon Court
Somers Town Estate (p 57):
Wolcot Street
Sidney Estate (p 55):
Sidney Street
Ampthill Square Estate (p 62):
Ampthill Square
Houghton Place
Mayford flats (p 64):
Crawley Mews
Cecil Rhodes House (p 66):
Chenies Place (pre-war)

Agar Grove Estate (p 860):
Elm Road
Wrotham Road (most)

Lost to schools

St Pancras National (p 30):
Southampton Crescent
Exmouth Street LCC (p 20):
Little Exmouth Street
Little George Street
Sir William Collins (p 49):
Barclay Street
St Mary & St Pancras (p 54):
Grenville Mews

From Hampstead Road to Euston Station

The first of our walks begins at Warren Street Station. Turn left outside the station and briefly bear left. The two-lane westbound carriageway in front of us reflects the original line and width of the 18th-century New Road (p 8). Cross to the bridge above the Euston Road underpass and look east (right) along **EUSTON ROAD**, here greatly widened in the 1960s. The tower of St Pancras New Church is visible in the distance.

The huge mirror-glass building, **No.250** Euston Road, housing Prudential Assurance (popularly called the Pru), was described by Pevsner as a "disturbing faceted cliff". Left of the Pru, **HAMPSTEAD ROAD** stretches away to the north. Properties at its south end were swept away in the building of the underpass. Where we stand was more or less the location of the Adam & Eve tavern which stood on the southwest corner of Hampstead Road. The southbound bridge across the underpass marks the site of the Old King's Head, its historic companion on the southeast corner. Just to its north, in 1797, the French writer and politician François Chateaubriand lodged at No.12 with Mrs O'Leary, an Irish widow, when he was a fugitive from the post-Revolutionary Terror.

Across Hampstead Road to the west looms Euston Tower, described in *From Primrose Hill to Euston Road*. North of the Pru is early-1980s housing, designed by Renton Howard Wood for Camden Council; just visible beyond is the distinctive white gable of the former Lord Palmerston public house (p 17).

Cross to the north side of Euston Road, and turn right, to the east side of Hampstead Road (here once known as Adam & Eve Row). Set back on the wide pavement is a cylindrical advertising display surmounted by a clock and temperature gauge, a product of the late 1990s. Here, until 1938, was the so-called 'Tottenham Court Road' terminus of the London Street Tramways, as near to the West End as the 'working-class' trams from Camden Road were allowed to penetrate.

We are now at or close to the site of Tottenham Court, the manor house of Tottenhall. Excavation of the Prudential site in 1979 yielded evidence of early Saxon and 13th- and 14th-century activity. Also found were remains of medieval and Tudor walls and a garderobe pit, part either of the manor house or of the adjoining Tudor farmhouse. The former has been depicted as a very slender building of timber and brick, standing in 1½ acres of ground with an orchard, and surrounded by a moat. A plan by William Necton dated 1591 shows the house as belonging to the Crown. Occupants included Daniel Clarke, Master Cook to Queen Elizabeth. The manor later passed into the hands of Charles Fitzroy, Lord Southampton (see p 11), in one corner of whose 'Southampton estate' the streets we are about to explore were first developed, mostly in the early 19th century.

The manor house – which was demolished in 1808 – was popularly known as 'King John's Palace', though there is no evidence that the Plantagenet king ever lived there. 'Palace Row' was the name once given to the adjoining section of the New Road, alongside which the Pru now stands. Previous occupants of this stretch of Euston Road included Maple's furniture makers, with repositories at Nos.262-270 (and at Nos.8–12 Hampstead Road) that had previously been occupied by the rival firm James Shoolbred. Another major local employer, Sangers the wholesale 'druggists', had premises at Nos.252–258 until the 1960s. Between Nos.270 & 272 was Mundy's Yard, home to an 'art metal factory' and the engineers' foundry of George Wailes & Co.; nearby, off Hampstead Road, was Grafton Yard. Also surviving until the road-widening were the Duke of Grafton pub at No.278 and the Orange Tree beyond, at the junction with North Gower Street (p 17). On the corner of Hampstead Road, a bank had long replaced the Old King's Head.

1 Tolmers Square Chapel

Though it is hard for us to imagine today, 18th-century Tottenham Court was a favourite rural retreat, with pleasant meadows and country lanes. At Easter and Whitsuntide the rural calm was shattered by the Tottenham Court Fair, which spread itself southward along Tottenham Court Road, then a lane lined by hawthorns. Notorious for its "vice and immorality", the fair featured bear-baiting, bull-fighting, penny theatres and boxing-booths (with female boxers); while "stalls of gooseberry-fool vied with 3d tea-booths". Suppressed by Parliament in 1808, the event was later revived as a slightly less rowdy Gooseberry Fair, centred on the Adam & Eve pub.

Walk briefly north up Hampstead Road and turn right into **TOLMERS SQUARE**. Pause in the central garden area. Tolmers was a hamlet near Cuffley (Herts.) at the source of a long-defunct branch of the New River. On the site of the square, the New River Company leased land in 1797 and built a reservoir to serve the West End; they later sank an artesian well. In 1848 a large range of baths and wash-houses was erected around three sides of the reservoir at its east end, with entrances in adjacent streets. Funded by voluntary contributions (with Prince Albert as patron and Lord Southampton as president), the baths catered for all classes. As well as first- and second-class cubicles for men and for women, there were

15

'vapour' and plunge baths. The charity also embarked on a programme of disinfecting the houses of the local poor.

The baths were demolished when, in 1863, the Square was laid out for housing. The present footway into Tolmers Square lies approximately on the line of the original road entrance from Hampstead Road. Stuccoed terraced houses, built by William Sawyer on the north and south sides of the new square, were intended to be more 'genteel' than those in the streets to the east. The 1871 census, however, reveals 364 people in the 28 houses, almost all of which were in multiple occupation; the Booth map of 1889 indicates "poverty and comfort mixed".

A Congregational Church was built in the centre of the Square at the same time as the houses (*Camden History Review* 24). A successor to an earlier 'Albany Chapel' in nearby Frederick Street (now Longford Street), it was designed by John Tarring (known as the "Gilbert Scott of the Non-Conformists") and boasted a 120-ft spire (Fig 1). The church was believed to be haunted after a minister had hanged himself, and strange lights were seen. When it eventually closed, in a remarkable change of use it became the Tolmer Cinema, opened in 1924 by George Smart; the spire survived for 4 more years. The building suffered bomb damage in 1944 and was bought by the Ponson family who, trading as New Tolmer Ltd, continued to run the cinema as a traditional, "popular and lively but not at all elegant" fleapit. In 1968, an application to rebuild the cinema was refused, as it would "prejudice an overall development scheme"; it closed in 1972.

During the 20th century half of the Square's south side was taken over by Sangers, the pharmaceutical company, and converted to factory or warehouse use. The Square became a *cause célèbre* in the 1970s, when the Tolmers Village Action Group and squatters led community opposition to the plans of property developer Joe Levy and his Stock Conversion Company for another Euston Tower-type development. For over a decade from 1962 Levy had bought properties in the area very cheaply. In September 1973, Camden decided to embark on a joint scheme with Stock Conversion, but a ratepayer immediately threatened the Council with a writ, and the following month many prominent Labour and trade union figures supported Tolmers Square residents against the scheme. The situation was resolved only with the passing of the Community Land Act 1975, which enabled Camden to purchase properties from Stock Conversion for £4 million.

The Square, as redeveloped for the Council in 1975–82 by Renton Howard Wood, is of a shape quite different from its predecessor: 4-storey houses and flats on the north and east sides, and the back of Hampstead Road housing on the west side have, as a focal point, two octagonal shapes: one is a grassy knoll (possibly recalling the old raised reservoir), the other a brick-paved sunken area. The **Square Tavern** was built as part of the development. The Square's traffic-free environment is enhanced by plane trees, rowans and shrubs.

We leave the Square through the arch on the north side. Immediately to our left is **FOUNDRY MEWS**, its name recalling the 19th-century foundries off Euston Road, including Wailes'. That engineering business had been started in 1825, at No.10 Palace Row (later No.258 Euston Road), by Charles Rich, an engineer, millwright and iron founder. After 1855 the business was carried on by George Wailes. Rex Wailes (a well-known writer on the history of engineering) was the last managing director of the business, which closed in 1960 when Euston Road was widened.

Emerge through a second arch into **DRUMMOND STREET**, built in the 1820s and here originally known as Charles Street East, probably in honour of Charles Fitzroy, 1st Baron Southampton. It was renamed in 1865 after Lady Caroline Drummond, a great-granddaughter of the 2nd Duke of Grafton. Pause here to survey the scene. Immediately opposite the prominent inscription the *Duke of Edinburgh* denotes a former late-Victorian beershop, named

Types amongst the 75 Camden History Society publications in print

Camden History Reviews (1975-present)

"Streets of" (historical surveys)
about all 13 districts of Camden

Wartime memories

Slums and near-slums

Restaurants and railways

Magistrates' courts

Historic and modern buildings

Cemeteries and funerary monuments

St Pancras and Camden Festivals

Painters (Constable and Morland)

DEAR READER ...

If you found this publication interesting and useful, you may be interested in joining the Camden History Society. Our activities include research, publication and lectures on all historical and social aspects of life in what is now the London Borough of Camden, including the historic boroughs that preceded it.

Membership benefits include receiving six issues of the *Newsletter* per year, the award-winning *Camden History Review* annually, monthly talks, the Annual Outing, and access to all publications (see reverse), complete list on application..

Membership is only £10 p.a.
Please fill in this form.

To: Dr Henry Fitzhugh, Membership Secretary, Camden History Society, 56 Argyle Street, London WC1H 8ER
Email: henryfitzhugh@talktalk.net

Subscription Rates are £10 p.a. for any grade of membership, including two people at the same address. Make cheques out to Camden History Society. Standing Order and Gift Aid forms are available.

_____
Name Mr/Mrs/Ms/Miss/Dr/Other (then CAPITALS, please)

_____
Address, with post code

_____

_____
Telephone

_____
Email

_____

as if it were a pub, a common practice at the time. It is now a café and a pharmacy. Also opposite, on the corner of Hampstead Road (left), is **Laurence Corner**, well known as an Army surplus store, but which also has a fancy-dress department. Its side wall bears a large mural. Facing this is another former pub, the Lord Palmerston, which now houses the **Camden People's Theatre**. The theatre began in October 1994, having broken away from the Unity Theatre (p 65), with the aim of working with "traditionally disenfranchised groups" and being affordable for local people. It has had help from the West Euston Partnership, and attracted funds from Sir John Gielgud, Bob Hoskins and large corporate organisations. Activities include outreach work with young people, a Pride Arts Festival, and productions ranging from Nabokov to Neil Simon (*Last of the Red Hot Lovers*). The Victorian Society campaigned in support of the Tolmers Village Action Group in preserving the buildings from **No.155** to the Lord Palmerston.

Almost opposite the exit from Foundry Mews is the entrance to **GEORGE MEWS**, comprising a delicate wrought-iron gateway, surmounted by a spearhead design and incorporating the name of the mews. Here, in the 19th century and at least until WW II, timber was stored and the yard variously served upholstery, furniture- and cabinet-making

factories in Hampstead Road. Disinfectant and battery factories and a printing works occupied the yard until 1960.

Drummond Street was previously home to a great variety of local shops and services, including Thomson's pawnbrokers at Nos.155–157. There were also small-scale manufacturing firms, including button makers and furniture makers. Nowadays, the street is renowned for its Indian restaurants, three of which are visible from where we stand. In 2001 many buildings were being renovated despite having been 'condemned' in reports supporting Levy's redevelopment plans, which were thwarted in part by widespread squatting during the 1970s.

Turn right along the south side of Drummond Street. No.153 is **Fred Tallant Hall** (*alias* 'The Meeting Place'), which serves both as the base of the London Esperanto Club, and as the regional office of the London CHA Club Ltd. Until his death in 1934, Fred Tallant was the Secretary of the London CHA Club, formed in Red Lion Square in 1901 as the Co-operative Holiday Association. The Club was one of seven organisations which founded the Federation of Rambling Clubs in 1905; it moved to this building in 1925.

Under the hall are two 'lifestyle' establishments: Planet Bazaar at **No.151** sells 1950s–1980s furniture and lighting;

while **No.145** offers Ayurvedic facelifts and other bodily rejuvenations. At first-floor level on **No.143** is a battered stone plaque bearing the inscription "Tolmers Square Institute & Schools" and to the right of the Gothic doorway of **No.141** is the foundation stone of the Institute, laid by Samuel Morley MP, a wealthy hosiery manufacturer who devoted £14,000 of his fortune to erecting chapels and who gave his name to Morley College in Lambeth. Once based in the Institute was the Euston Middle Class School for Girls, founded in 1880; another of Frederick Waymouth's short-lived 'collegiate' schools, the slightly earlier Euston College for Boys, was nearby George Street (see *Camden History Review* 24).

At the junction with **NORTH GOWER STREET** cross the street left and walk northwards. Note the painted sign "Gower Street" on **No.211**. The street was originally called George Street, probably after George, 2nd Baron Southampton, but renamed in 1937 as a northern continuation of Bloomsbury's Gower Street. The 'North' prefix was added to the name in 1968, after the Euston Road underpass severed the two parts of the street, but the 3-digit Gower Street house numbers were retained. Most of the buildings are listed, being noteworthy for the variety of their balcony and railing designs. The **North Gower Hotel** at Nos.190–198 opposite was once five houses. As a London Borough of Camden green plaque testifies, **No.200** was the workplace of Lord Pitt of Hampstead (1913–94), the West Indian physician and civil rights campaigner, whose surgery occupied the ground floor from 1950 for 34 years. The basement served, in 1959–60, as the HQ of the fledgling Anti-Apartheid Movement.

Pause to look down the next turning on the right. Originally Exmouth Street, after Admiral Lord Exmouth, a hero of the Napoleonic Wars, it was renamed **STARCROSS STREET** in 1937 after a Devonshire village facing the *town* of Exmouth across the Exe estuary. Connolly's (Blackley) Ltd, an independent subsidiary of British Associated Callenders Cables Ltd (BICC), had a well-established association with the area, with a warehouse and storage at No.23. The firm was not allowed to redevelop, even though it had an important export role and there was vacant land available. Although the local Initial Development Plan of the 1950s had zoned the area for commerce and permitted the development of warehouses, repositories and wholesale trade, the Plan was amended in the 1960s to be zoned as 'West End'. The small modern brick building with the awning is the entrance to the **Shahjalal Jame Masjid Euston Mosque** on the corner (at No.204A North

Gower Street). The remainder of the south side of Starcross Street comprises two ranges of 4-storey terraces in differently coloured bricks, another of Renton Howard Wood's attractive developments for Camden Council.

On the north side, the former Exmouth Street elementary **school** was opened by the LCC in 1916, with separate departments for boys, girls and infants. This building continues in educational use. At various times it has been the LCC Starcross School (for 'senior girls'), and a branch of Princeton College (Camden's college of further education until it merged with Kingsway College). It is now the 'lower school' annexe of the Maria Fidelis convent (p 38).

Next on our left, almost opposite Starcross Street, is another way into George Mews; the road has been paved with bricks which echo those of the flats at its north end, part of the 1980s Hampstead Road development. On the south corner of the Mews, **Nos.231–233 North Gower Street** is a post-WW II office block which blends with both its Georgian and newer neighbours.

The northernmost section of North Gower Street is pedestrianised. On our left, at **Nos.235–295**, is more of the 1980s council development. On the wall opposite, an attractive mural has been painted by pupils of Maria Fidelis and South Camden Community Schools and

children from the (Bengali) Surma Centre. It was funded by the local organisations Groundwork Camden, West Euston Partnership, and Community Chest; artists Kay Stark and Leanne Turvey co-ordinated the work. Look back to take in the vista southwards along Gower Street into Bloomsbury.

Continue and arrive again at **HAMPSTEAD ROAD**, where an old St Pancras lamppost is a rare survival. The stretch of road south (left) from here once boasted a great variety of useful shops, including T Boocock, draper at Nos.52–58. In the 1980s housing development only one shop was provided on this side of the road, **No.100 Hampstead Road**, now the Euston Saree Centre.

Turn right (north) along the main road, past red-brick **No.108**, built as the St Pancras Female Charity School, a girls' orphanage. Its foundation stone was laid in 1904 by Lord Southampton (the ground landlord) and the Vicar of St Pancras, the Rev. Henry Luke Paget. The architects were E W Hudson and S G Goss. The building (with the former Temperance Hospital complex beyond) is now part of the headquarters of the Camden & Islington Health Services NHS Trust; it houses the Margarete Centre which runs health clinics.

A broad path on the right between No.108 and what was originally known as the Temperance Hospital leads us into

St James' Gardens. A tablet on the right-hand wall recalls the opening of gardens in 1887 by Olive, wife of Henry Lawson Webster Lawson, Liberal MP for St Pancras West from 1885 until 1892. Subsequently, as Viscount Burnham, Lawson was Chairman of the Standing Joint Committee of Teachers and Local Education Authorities and formulated the Burnham Scales for teachers' pay. Among other worthies listed is Frederick Purchese, who was Deputy Chairman of the St Pancras Vestry's Highways and Public Works Committee.

The gardens were originally the overspill burial ground of St James's, Piccadilly. Its chapel, St James's Hampstead Road, which backed on to the ground, stood on the site of the Temperance Hospital courtyard (see *From Primrose Hill to Euston Road*). Designed by Thomas Hardwick and consecrated in 1791, it was demolished only in 1956. Most of the burial ground's gravestones were moved to the perimeter, where a few survive.

The first monument we encounter is an obelisk topped with a Celtic cross in memory, first, of Edward Christie, a midshipman of HMS Theseus, who died in 1803 aged 19 at Port Royal, Jamaica, on board a captured slave ship. The back of the memorial commemorates Captain Charles Christie, who was later killed on active service in Persia. Civilian members

of the Christie family, who were West End residents, are commemorated on the sides of the memorial.

Take the winding path to the left of the cross, past a handful of mainly illegible tombstones. Other notables buried here include the explorer Matthew Flinders; the artist George Morland and his wife; John Hoppner, the portrait painter; and Lord George Gordon, infamous for inciting the eponymous riots. A local worthy also buried here was John Leverton, founder of the funeral undertakers (p 72), who died in 1843 aged 80.

The large brick building adjoining the gardens to the south is the back of a former London & North West Railway (LNWR) building in Cobourg Street (p 20). Ahead of us is the west side of Euston Station, a monotonous corrugated metal and brick construction in **CARDINGTON STREET**. The street marked the boundary with the Duke of Bedford's property in this area: Cardington had been added by John, 4th Duke, to his Bedfordshire lands.

On reaching the entrance to the garden look left up Cardington Street to where it bends round westward to join Hampstead Road, near the site of the turnpike shown in a cartoon of 1798 by Rowlandson. Along this stretch is the **Thistle Euston** (formerly Kennedy) **Hotel**, whose nearest corner is flanked by four attractive Victorian lampposts. The hotel supplanted

the longstanding, war-damaged, printing works of McCorquedale. Cardington Street was once renowned for the production of stained glass windows: Abate & Clerville and Clayton & Bell at No.24a were joined by Heaton & Butler c.1858. During the 19th century, Birchmore Terrace (probably named after an 1850s St Pancras Vestry Relieving Officer) was a small cul-de-sac off the north side of the street, extinguished by the encroachment of railway carriage sheds. The original Cardington Street ran west–east from Hampstead Road to a right-angled junction with long-lost Whittlebury Street. "Ranger of Whittlebury Forest" was among the hereditary titles of the Dukes of Grafton; Whittlebury Lodge (Northants.) was the Fitzroy family's second home. The street, which ran north–south, was demolished in the 1870s, to make way for a westward extension of Euston Station, in the construction of which the eastern side of St James' Gardens was also lost. The 1871 census gives a picture of residents of the former street: those who were not railway employees plied a great variety of trades. There was a pub at No.41, the Southampton Arms.

Turn right along the present main section of Cardington Street. Note the attractive railings of the garden, before we reach the **Hotel Ibis** (right). In 1987 this was the first newly built hotel in central London for 10 years. Originally to have been called Hotel Euston, it is typical of 1980s design. 19th-century coffins from the former St James's Churchyard were discovered when the foundations were dug.

We now reach Drummond Street. On the opposite corner, at the north end of Melton Street (p 23), are the distinctive arches and ox-blood-red tiles of the former Euston station for the Charing Cross, Euston & Hampstead Railway, opened in 1907, known once as the 'Hampstead Tube' and now the Charing Cross branch of the Northern Line. This separate surface building in Melton Street was not used for long: it was closed in 1914, together with the City branch station in what is now Eversholt Street (p 30); since then both branches of the line have been served by a combined station beneath the mainline station. The old station building now houses an electricity substation.

Before the redevelopment of Euston Station, **DRUMMOND STREET** continued east across the station site to Eversholt Street, and beyond it to Churchway (p 32). Turn right and west along the surviving part of the street. We are following in the footsteps of Charles Dickens, who once walked this way to school at Wellington House Academy in Hampstead Road. Here in Drummond Street Charles and his school chums would amuse themselves by pretending to be beggars, asking old ladies for charity, then running away laughing at their victims'

surprise. In *Sketches by Boz*, Miss Amelia Martin, *The mistaken milliner*, lived at No.47.

Turn right into **COBOURG STREET**, long spelt elsewhere without the middle 'o', and built as a mainly residential street in 1816, the year in which Princess Charlotte married Leopold of Saxe-Coburg. At the far end is **No.1**, the back of which we noticed from St James' Gardens, and which started life as horse stables for the railway company. It now houses the architectural practice Jestico & Whiles, which has sympathetically renovated the building. The Cobourg Street building was previously home to Collectors' Corner, which sold railway memorabilia and had its entrance in Cardington Street; it has since moved to the National Railway Museum, in York.

To the left of No.1 is evidence of the line of former Little George Street; once running diagonally north-west from here to join North Gower Street until it was destroyed in the building of the Exmouth Street School. Both Little George Street and nearby Little Exmouth Street were indicated on the Booth map as being of the poorest class. On the corner with Starcross Street, and preserving the street's original name, is the **Exmouth Arms**, a post-WW II rebuild of a war-damaged pub. In the late 19th century, the street was home to a dairy at No.20, complete with cowsheds behind, run by one J F Ward. Retrace your steps down Cobourg

Street, passing, on the right, more examples of 1970s Renton Howard Wood housing.

On regaining Drummond Street, continue west (right) along it. Off this north side is **EXMOUTH MEWS**, providing access to the housing in Starcross and Cobourg Streets. A little further on and accessed through a square-cut opening is **CHARLES PLACE**, originally a turning off Charles Street East. Among the businesses that once thrived here were timber storage, cabinet making, engineering, and stained-glass painting. On the opposite side of the street are more of the restaurants for which Drummond Street is now noted: at **No.121** is the Diwana Bhel Poori (opened 1972), renowned for its Indian vegetarian cuisine. The shop at **No.115** displays good examples of the extensive range of food and spices sold in the street.

At the **Crown & Anchor**, a Listed building dating from the 1820s, we regain **NORTH GOWER STREET**. On the southwest corner opposite, at **Nos.203–209**, is Al-Ahram House, the London office of the prestigious Cairo-based Arab newspaper. Sharing the premises is the Compass Partnership, providers of consultancy services to charities and voluntary-sector organisations. As Drummond House, the building was previously occupied by offices of the Transport & General Workers' Union.

Turn left along the east side of the street. Listed **Nos.184–188**, in yellow stock brick, are noted for their cast-iron balconies and railings with flambé finials, and form an attractive group with the Crown & Anchor. The narrow glass-plated front of Mediacom (a subsidiary of Grey Advertising) at **No.180** marks the entrance to a former sawmill.

Pause at the corner (with Euston Street) to look at the opposite side of the street. **No.195** might easily be dismissed as routine 1960s, but in fact it dates from 1938–9. A building ahead of its time, it was designed by Maxwell Fry (a specialist in social housing), its blue panels a then innovative use of colour. The block was built as one of several hostels for homeless young women run by Cecil Houses (Inc), a charity founded (in Boswell Street, Holborn) in 1926–7 by Mrs Cecil Chesterton, journalist, drama critic and author of *In Darkest London*. The building is now a University College (UCL) hall of residence named **Prankerd House**, presumably after Professor Thomas Prankerd, clinical haematologist, author of *The Red Cell*, and a former Dean of the College's Medical School.

Beyond the paved entrance into Tolmers Square, original early 19th-century houses survive at **Nos.185–191** and are Grade II Listed. Nos.183–185 bear a blue LCC plaque to Giuseppe Mazzini. The exiled Italian patriot lodged here when he first arrived in London in 1837 and was working as a journalist. At the end of the street is the unattractive rear of the Pru building (p 14).

Turn left into **EUSTON STREET**. On the left at **No.100** is the Copyright Libraries Agency, formerly the British Library's Copyright Deposit Office, to which copies of every publication in Britain (including this one!) are still sent for legal deposit in the five other designated copyright libraries. Further along this side are more Renton Howard Wood houses. At **Nos.81–103** opposite is the Methodist International Centre. Originally completed in 1939 to the designs of architects Munby & Smith, it housed the laboratories and offices of the British Non-Ferrous Metals Association until 1974, when the latter moved to Bayswater. Across Cobourg Street is the **Jolly Gardeners**; a pub of this name has been here from when the area was first built up. The name may recall the several nursery gardens which previously lined the nearby New Road (see p 8).

Cross Euston Street and turn down L-shaped **REGNART BUILDINGS**, originally Southampton Buildings and renamed after either Sir Horace Grece Regnart or Clare Henry Regnart: both were presidents of Maple's, the furniture-makers, who had a factory in Stephenson Way (p 22). Continue a few paces to view 4- and 5-storey converted brick warehouses with a mix of offices and apartments. A National School is known to have been on the site in 1835.

Return to Euston Street and continue east (right). More Renton Howard Wood housing is opposite at **Nos.58–64**, and beyond at **Nos.54–56** is a striking 3-storey building with grey metal bay windows on the first floor.

Pause by the **Cottage Hotel** at No.71, an early 19th-century building which has been heavily restored. On the corner is a St Pancras Borough Council bollard, some 4 ft high. Ahead of us is **Euston Station Colonnade**, which marks the line of an extinct eastern section of Euston Street. Facing onto the north side of that stretch until demolished in 1937 was the attractive Euston Crescent, which comprised 17 houses with handsome railings. Euston Street was named Crescent Street until 1867, because it linked Euston Crescent and the south-facing Seymour Crescent, pulled down earlier to make way for a hotel. There was originally yet another crescent, Southampton Crescent, to the east, off the north side of what is now Lancing Street (p 30). The sections of Euston and Drummond Streets that were south of the station were serviced by two former mews: Melton Mews off Melton Street, and Seymour Row (Euston Mews until 1886) off former Seymour Street (p 30).

Turn right into another L-shaped

street, **STEPHENSON WAY**, named after Robert Stephenson, chief engineer of the LNWR for which Euston was the London terminal. Its now rather bleak north–south section was originally called Little Crescent Street because of its proximity to Crescent Street (see above); it is still partly cobbled, but with patches of tarmac. On the right UCL's **Wolfson House**, a 1970s office building of brick and concrete, houses some College departments. The road turns right; this east–west stretch was originally called Southampton Mews and became Euston Buildings in 1882. Seven blocks of working-class housing were erected on its south side, named after royal dukes, and owned by the Castle Martin Trust. On their site today is the back of the former Cambridge University Press block in Euston Road (see below), which retains the publisher's coat of arms. Opposite are two new buildings of contrasting designs, which nicely complement each other. **No.12**, the home of the Magic Circle since 1998, displays a flag bearing the signs of the zodiac. **No.14**, by Jestico & Whiles and their previous offices from 1986 until 1998, now houses Gross Fine, surveyors and property managers, and incorporates a modern version of a taking-in door. The rear of No.210 Euston Road has inoffensive two-tone beige cladding. Stephenson Way is home to some well-known voluntary sector organisations: at

No.18 is Arthritis Care, while **Nos.24–32**, the Charity Centre, which was Maple's bedding factory until its closure in 1972, houses the Institute of Family Therapy, various mediating bodies and the National Training Organisation, plus the Directory of Social Change, which from small beginnings in Hampstead in the 1970s now runs major conferences and a specialist bookshop.

On regaining North Gower Street, turn left to pass the **Euston Square Hotel**, where ironwork supporting the entrance canopy and the railings have been preserved. The hotel was previously the Gower Hostel of University College Hospital.

We now turn left into **EUSTON ROAD** (see also pp 31 & 42). **Euston Square** [Underground] **Station**, which was opened on the Metropolitan Railway in 1863, was more appropriately named Gower Street Station until 1909. Entrances to the station from both sides of the road also serve as a public subway, but we stay on this side of the road (the opposite, south, side is described in *Streets of Bloomsbury & Fitzrovia*). The pavement ahead, with roadside bollards to prevent parking, is spacious, indicative of the original frontages to properties when the New Road was first developed. Nos.18–19 Southampton Place (as this stretch was then known) served as studios of the 19th-century engravers Edward and William

Finden. Some original houses, with garden plots in front, still stood in 1945.

No.222, the MRC Clinical Trials Building, was refurbished in the 1980s. Built by Moiret & Wood in 1954–8, it was formerly the headquarters of the National Union of Mineworkers (NUM), until the union's decision to relocate to Sheffield in the late 1980s, taking with them the sculptures and mirrors which had adorned the façade. Clad with grey and beige marble, the Two Ten science and arts gallery at **No.210** is run by the Wellcome Trust and hosts temporary exhibitions. A previous building at **No.200** was where the London Female Preventive and Reformatory Institution ran a reformatory home from 1858 until 1907. The present No.200 is Portland stone-fronted Bentley House, built in the late 1930s as the London base of Cambridge University Press (CUP); the architects were W Curtis Green, RA, Son and Lloyd. It was renovated in 1990, the name being retained (Cambridge University gave one Richard Bentley a free hand in setting up the Press at the end of the 17th century). CUP moved out at the end of the 1970s. The NUR (now RMT) used the premises during the rebuilding (opposite) of its 'Unity House' headquarters, short-lived and now demolished, following the union's removal to Chalton Street (p 40). No.200 is now occupied by the Wellcome Trust. Its design was influenced by that of its neighbour at **No.194**, built in 1932 by W H Gunton. With giant Ionic columns, it has long been a local office of the War Pensions Agency and its predecessors, including the interestingly named National Amalgamated Approval Society.

We reach the junction with **MELTON STREET**, a late Georgian name of unknown origin. Cross with care at the pelican crossing. Pause here to look back along the west side of the street, opposite. **No.1** (with No.194 Euston Road) has interesting railings, and was built in a strange mixture of Classical styles suggestive of unimplemented Edwardian ideas for the redesign of Euston Station. Originally the London, Edinburgh and Glasgow Assurance Building, it was built in Bath stone c.1907 to the design of Beresford Pite, and is Listed also for its wrought iron railings. **No.10**, of the 1960s but inoffensive, is the headquarters of the Transport Salaried Staffs Association (TSSA), the white-collar rail union. It also has a conference centre for Age Concern. A public house on the street's east side, the Euston Arms at No.31, survived until at least 1961.

The green space we have reached is **EUSTON SQUARE**. Begun c.1811, it was designed as the centrepiece of Lord Southampton's local development, and as a northward extension to Bloomsbury. Previously occupying the site of the square was a large nursery garden, latterly known as Montgomery's Nursery. On its north side, in a 'pretty' little house called Montgomery Cottage, John Wolcot, better known as the political satirist Peter Pindar, died in 1819, penniless and partially blind.

The square extended on both sides of Euston Road until 1879, when its southern half was renamed Endsleigh Gardens. The railings around the present square and fronting Euston Road are original (and Listed), although some are damaged. Other than Nos.70–71 (p 31), the square's original real estate has not survived, most having been demolished in 1937, probably to make way for a proposed rebuilding of Euston Station which did not materialise.

On the north side once stood distinguished Regency stuccoed and pilastered terraces of c.1811 designed by either C A Busby or James Burton. These two blocks of 15 and 13 houses (separated by Euston Grove) were built by Thomas Jennings of Upper Marchmont Street and by John Knight of Kenton Street. At first-floor level were French windows with roofed balconies 'of exceptionally beautiful design'. In its heyday, the Square had many distinguished residents and attracted many clergymen, including the Rev. Henry Stebbing, the incumbent of St James's, Hampstead Road, who lived at No.16 (1836–58). No.23 was home to Thomas Hancock Nunn, a pioneer of social work. Thomas Leigh Hunt, a journalist writing for the *Spectator*, *Morning Chronicle* and *Daily Telegraph* and eldest son of the essayist-poet, lived at No.6 (1863–5) and at No.26 (1866–72). John Payne Collier was a Shakespearean critic who also rescued many famous authors from oblivion: he was responsible for an outstanding edition of the works of Edmund Spenser. However, this resident of No.25 (1834–9) was at other times something of a rogue, forging works of Shakespeare, *inter alia*. His work led to his appointment as secretary to a royal commission on the British Museum. Sir Claudius Stephen Hunter, a relative of Sir Hans Sloane, lived at No.23 (1838–51): he was a solicitor and City alderman, who served successively as Sheriff and Lord Mayor.

On the west side of the square, No.30 was home to the scientific writer Charles Tomlinson, a lecturer at UCL who in 1838 published *The Student's Manual of Natural Philosophy*. Next door at No.31 lived George Bullen, keeper of printed books at the British Museum; his house would later become the Griffins Hotel. William Inwood, joint architect of the new parish church, lived at No.62 in 1822–36, while his neighbour at No.70 was printer and publisher Richard Gilbert, whose *Clerical Guide* or *Ecclesiastical Directory* of 1817 was a forerunner of Crockford's annual directory.

Take the path leading diagonally towards the main line station, past a seat commemorating the Queen's Silver Jubilee in 1977. Turn left up a ramp leading to a brick-paved area; here plane trees relieve the tedium of the Grant Thornton and Railtrack office blocks. These are two of a group of three squat towers, finished in grey-tinted glass and clad in South African polished black marble, to designs by Richard Seifert (1910–2001). The original plan was for four taller blocks, but the GLC placed restrictions on both their height and the area of office space to be allowed. Construction began in 1974; the original freeholders British Rail gained an annual rental of £3m from Fluor (a Californian oil engineering service company) in 1978. By the end of the century, rental income to Railtrack amounted to £6.5m. Walk towards the 3-storey offices, of a slightly more interesting design, which straddle the bus station area in front of the rail station.

We reach the strange metallic shape of *Piscator*, sculpted by Eduardo Paolozzi (with Ray Watson), and cast by the iron founders Robert Taylor & Co. The 16-ton, galvanised painted, cast-iron sculpture was erected on its black marble plinth in 1981, commissioned by the British Railways Board and others. *Piscator* (Latin for 'fisherman') is intended to represent a man's head and shoulders, symbolising how our society is affected by the machine. The sculpture was originally known as *The Euston Head*.

Bearing right, descend a few shallow steps. Ahead, a depression in the ground on this part of the Euston Square green space, and the top of an arch carrying the roadway to our left, are evidence that the two halves of the Square were once linked by a pedestrian tunnel under Euston Grove. During the 1920s, the railway company lent the Square to the St Pancras House of Fellowship (affiliated to the Shaftesbury Society), which here ran an open-air school for delicate children drawn from neighbouring schools. During WW II the Open Air Centre continued to provide educational classes, activities such as Girl Guides and Junior Women's Air Corps, and health services (e.g. immunisation). The Fellowship's Chair of Council was Miss Edith Neville (see p 49), well known for her work with the St Pancras Housing Association.

To our left is the bus station, with **EUSTON GROVE** running south into Euston Road. The road required an Act of Parliament in 1869 for the LNWR to acquire this land from Lord Southampton, and to build the 80-foot-wide drive flanked by the two lodges on Euston Road (to our right). Designed by the LNWR architect J B Stansby, these are the only buildings that remain from the old Euston Station as finally conceived. Each lodge is of two storeys, square in plan, faced with Portland stone, and with a low-pitched lead-covered roof. The quoin stones bear the names of

stations then served by the railway. In the north and south pediments are sculptures by Joseph Pitts representing England, Scotland, Wales and Ireland.

In recent years, the road leading into the bus station has been surfaced pleasingly with brick in various shades, with raised granite sett road humps. The lampposts resemble jousting lances, and each is surmounted by a laurel wreath and helmet at lamp level.

Cross to the **War Memorial**, designed by Reginald Wynn Owen and unveiled in October 1921 by Lord Haig, which commemorates the 3,719 men of the LNWR who fell in WW I, including 3 VCs and 950 who gained other honours. The stone obelisk on a granite base is flanked by four bronze figures representing the Navy, Air Force, Infantry and Artillery. Looking east from the War Memorial, at the other end of the bus station, is the **Head of Steam** pub, popular with train-spotters for its railway memorabilia.

Cross the road, under the "bridge" building straddling the bus station, to emerge into what might charitably be described as a piazza that fronts the station. On the base of the left-hand shrub planter is a plaque to commemorate the inauguration in 1979 – more than 2 years late – of the Bloomsbury section of the Silver Jubilee Walkway, by the patron of the Walkway Trust, the Duke of Gloucester (a practising architect).

The **statue of Robert Stephenson** (Fig 2), the engineer and main player in the railway company and station, now stands on a raised area at the end of the piazza to the right. In bronze and on a plinth of Aberdeen granite, Baron Carlo Marochetti's work originally stood between the two Euston Road lodges, and had been presented by the Institution of Civil Engineers. Marochetti is noted for the realism with which he sculpted his subjects' clothing; you may even glimpse daylight below the insteps of Stephenson's shoes. The aforementioned raised area was previously an 'ornamental pool', never very

2   Euston Grove with Marochettti's statue of Robert Stephenson (1939)

3 The Euston Arch or propylaeum
(photograph c.1900) with horse cabs

savoury, and constantly strewn with tin cans. One spring in the 1980s, a family of mallard ducklings took up residence with their parents; sadly, they did not long survive in this inhospitable habitat. The two tall, dark concrete structures conceal ventilation shafts for the Underground station.

The strange tripods in the middle of the piazza are **Euston Banners** by Sue Ridge and Mark Firth, which were erected in 1994. The banners represent the colours of Henry Charles Fitzroy, 1st Earl of Euston (the second natural son of Charles II by Barbara Villiers), and incorporate the chequered baton sinister, denoting illegitimacy. Euston Station was built on property owned by the Fitzroy family (and named after their country seat at Euston in Suffolk). The four low stone benches close to the *Banners* were commissioned in 1990 by British Rail's Public Art Development Trust for the Gateshead Garden Festival. The benches, by Paul de Monchaux, were installed at Euston in 1993. Each is in a different type of stone, and has an inscription beneath, indicating the stone's age, provenance and geological period. You may wish to rest on one of them or on a wooden bench hereabouts to consider the history of the area.

Before the present rebuilding of Euston Station, Euston Grove was a residential street that continued northwards to meet Drummond Street. No.2 was home to two eminent people of the 19th century. John Cooper, an actor very much in vogue for his Shakespearean roles at Drury Lane, lived there 1845–53. The comparative anatomist Robert Edmond Grant, a friend of Charles Darwin and Professor of Zoology at UCL, was a resident 1858–74.

North of Euston Street, and thus on the site of the present station concourse, Euston Grove opened out into Euston Place. This was lined on either side by the first two railway hotels ever built, in 1839, to the designs of Philip Hardwick. The Victoria opened at first as a dormitory, serving breakfast only, under the management of a former steward of the Athenaeum; bedrooms cost from 3s.6d. to 5s. per night (£0.17 to £0.25). The Adelaide, later called the Euston, was a more conventional hotel. In 1881, the two hotels amalgamated, and were connected in the 'modern French style' by a screen across Euston Grove, designed by Stansby with details by J McLaren. The hotel closed in 1962 and was demolished to make way for the rebuilding of Euston Station. Seven of the eight other properties in the street were private hotels – including Giffards at No.1 and the West Riding Hotel at No.4 – which also survived until the early 1960s.

On the other side of Drummond Street (on a line beyond the modern concourse), you would have arrived at the Euston 'Arch' (Fig 3), more correctly a Propylaeum, the design of which was inspired by that on the Acropolis in Athens. Arthur Mee called it one of the grandest English specimens of the Greek style. Built of Bramley Fall stone in 1838, it was immense – 72 1/2ft high; its four columns were London's tallest (44ft 2in) and hollow. There was a chamber in the roof, providing very cramped office space, reached by spiral staircases in one corner. Cast-iron gates decorated with the company's coat of arms (one of which is now on display at the National Railway Museum in York), designed by Philip Hardwick and manufactured by J J Bramah, marked the entry into the station. On either side of the arch were four pavilions or lodges, not as attractive as those facing Euston Road.

The Arch was restored and the station's name was carved on the architrave in 1870. Eleven years later, construction of railway offices destroyed the western lodge. The Arch gradually became surrounded by buildings, and its grandeur could no longer be fully appreciated.

The original plans for the 1960s rebuilding of the station included retention of the Arch. However, the LCC had no objection to its demolition, provided that it was erected elsewhere "in an appropriate, dignified and open setting"; the British Transport Commission estimated the cost for this at £180,000 (later increased to £190,000)). Woodrow Wyatt MP asked questions in Parliament of the Minister of Housing Local Government, Sir Keith Joseph. Other expressions of concern came from the Royal Fine Arts Commission. Nevertheless, the fate of the Arch assumed a kind of inevitability, and demolition – Britain's "worst act of corporate vandalism" – began on 6 November 1961; 3 months later, nothing remained. Mr Valori, the demolition contractor, so hated the job that he offered to number the stones and re-erect them on BR land elsewhere, but to no avail. In place of the Arch today we have the train indicator board of the rebuilt **Euston Station**.

The proposal for the original station and the London & Birmingham Railway – the first trunk line into London – passed as an Act in May 1833, after initial objections from the House of Lords. At first known as 'Euston Square', the station opened in 1837. Based around the present platform 6, it was planned by Robert Stephenson. The platform sheds were designed by Sir Charles Fox, and featured a colonnade of Doric columns in cast-iron and iron roofs, a first in railway architecture. For the first 8 years, cables powered by a condensing engine hauled carriages up the incline to Chalk Farm, where a locomotive was attached. Queen Victoria and Prince Albert made their first northbound train journey from Euston in 1844.

Two years later, the London & Birmingham Railway merged with two other lines to form the LNWR. A large group of new buildings was proposed, designed on a Roman Bath model, and comprising a great hall, a grand staircase, meeting room, board room, general offices, and new booking offices. The board room was graced by busts of both George and Robert Stephenson and of fellow engineer Joseph Locke, Robert's collaborator in the building of the railway. Philip Hardwick was the architect, but the work was carried out 1846–9 by his son, Philip Charles Hardwick. The glorious Great Hall was inspired by the principal apartment in Peruzzi's Palazzo Massimo alle Colonne in Rome. Relief panels depicting the railway's various destinations and a representation of Britannia, accompanied by a lion, a ship, the Arts and Sciences and Mercury, were designed by John Thomas (1813–63). The Hall's walls were finished in grey Martin's cement, painted to imitate granite. Columns were finished in red granite, with white marble caps and bases. Around the sides of the Hall later stood coin-activated models of engines enclosed in glass cases. Surveying the scene was a second Stephenson statue, of 1852, this one depicting George, the engineer father of Robert, and sculpted in Carrara marble by E H Baily; it is now at the NRM in York. In 1912, the booking hall incorporated refreshment and dining rooms. In 1916 Lutyens advised on the redecoration of the walls of the Hall, which were painted in white and gold. A previous offer by G F Watts to paint frescoes for nothing had been turned down.

At the same time as the acquisition of land to the south, the station was extended east in 1869–70. Some properties in former Seymour Street (p 30) and the 1836–37 carriage sheds were demolished to make way for the construction of Arrival Platforms 1–3. The company's then engineer, William Baker, raised the roof-line by introducing cast-iron pillars. The expansion of the station continued apace in the 1880s, first with new offices in Drummond Street, finished in grey cement and stone, by architects Joseph & Smithern. At the same time, the Parliamentary powers to extend the station west to diverted Cardington Street enabled Platforms 12–15 to be built; they opened in 1892. Signal box Euston No.2, brought into use in April 1891, was the largest of its kind in existence.

For at least 50 years there were plans to redevelop or rebuild Euston Station. An obscure Edwardian scheme came to nothing. Few details are known of a later plan in 1935, under which the station would have resembled a 1930s cinema! Stone for the building would have come from the Caldon Low Quarries in Staffordshire. The Doric arch would have disappeared with that scheme, too, but on that occasion it was saved. The scheme may have been shelved because of poor financial results for the railway company in 1938, after which WW II intervened.

The impetus for the present station was the electrification of the West Coast Main Line out of Euston, for which building began in 1962. Hardwick's architecture "on the grandest scale" was swept away "in the interests of modernity" (Pevsner). British Rail's London Midland Regional Architect, R L Moorcroft, produced a stark, utilitarian building, using the black polished granite and white mosaic finishes so beloved of 1960s architects. Built by Taylor Woodrow, it was opened by the Queen in October 1968.

Now enter the station. Despite an adequate number of retail premises and other facilities in the station's precinct (including the under-used colonnades on either side), Railtrack has cluttered the Passenger Hall with small shops, which have the effect of obliterating the daylight while still leaving the station without adequate seating. To the left of the Passenger Hall, the Travel Centre was an innovation: this area includes the booking offices and facilities for reservations and enquiries. It has quite an interesting moulded ceiling, akin to very regular small stalactites.

If you travel home by Tube, further reminders of the area's past may await you in Euston's Underground, reached from the Passenger Hall. On the Northern Line

(Platforms 1 & 2), the platform walls, reclad in 1987 (to designs by David Hamilton and Robert Cooper) incorporate, like the *Euston Banners*, the colours of the Fitzroy coat-of-arms, together with images of the same and an eloquent explanation of their local significance. On the Victoria Line platforms (as at all stations on the line), each seat recess sports a tiled motif. Here at Euston, Tom Eckersley's design offers us a reminder of the Doric Arch, whose senseless destruction came to symbolise a turning point in town planning and conservation, and changes in attitudes to our historic buildings.

Route 2
Somers Town (south & west)

This walk takes you across land that was once a farm known as The Brill, part of the Lay Manor of St Pancras, belonging to Charterhouse. After the Dissolution it passed through various hands, being sold in 1628 to one Charles Cocks of the Middle Temple. In the following century it ended up in the hands of a later Charles Cocks whose grandson (great-nephew of the 18th-century Lord Chancellor Somers) was in 1784 created Baron Somers of Evesham. Inspired by the expansion of London and realising the advantages of the New Road which ran across a corner of his estate, Baron Somers sought to develop his land for building and leased it in 1783 to Jacob Leroux, architect and Middlesex JP. Leroux set about creating a kind of self-contained suburban village, which was to become known as Somers Town. Within two decades its pleasant back gardens had been built over and Somers Town soon deteriorated into one of London's most notorious slums, which were however never picturesque enough to attract the attention of chroniclers or illustrators of the time. It is mentioned by former resident Dickens, but merely as a source of clerks pouring out daily to City offices.

If arriving by Tube, walk through the Euston Station concourse to the easternmost exit to the right of W H Smith's. As you approach the steps leading to Eversholt Street you glimpse distant views of the pinnacled towers of St Pancras Chambers, flanked by the contrasting square brick tower of its neighbour, the British Library. Both St Pancras and Euston stations have had a huge influence on the part of Somers Town we are about to explore. Pause briefly at the top of the steps to view a section of **EVERSHOLT STREET**, known before 1938 as Seymour Street (Frances, the second wife of George 2nd Baron Southampton, was the daughter of Lord Robert Seymour). We have yet to reach Somers Town proper, and are on the eastern edge of the old Grafton-Southampton estate. Several streets hereabouts were therefore given Fitzroy family or country estate names.

The large block opposite and to the left is **Euston House**, built in 1934 to designs by W H Hamlyn and A V Heal as the headquarters of the London Midland and Scottish Railway Company, subsequently the HQ of British Rail. Since privatisation it has housed the IT training company Learning Tree International and the Wellcome Institute for the History of Medicine, a branch of the ubiquitous pharmaceutical giant Glaxo-Wellcome,

another dominant presence in the area around Euston. Architecturally hardly worth a glance, the building's only feature of interest is a relief of railway features at the top – you may need binoculars to see it. One of the buildings demolished to make way for Euston House was the surface building for one of Euston's two Underground stations (see also p 20). This little ornamental green-and-white tiled building, designed by the architect known as S R J 'Tate Gallery' Smith, belonged to the pioneering City and South London line, the world's first underground railway run by electricity. Also the first deep-level true 'tube' railway, it was extended to Euston in 1907; by 1914 the station was out of use and the line is now incorporated into the City branch of the Northern line.

The little street opposite is **LANCING STREET**, originally known as Southampton Street. Several streets in the area were renamed in the 1860s after various seaside towns. The playground visible at the end marks the site of the Anglican St Pancras National Schools. They were built in 1837 to a design by Charles Inwood, whose father and brother were the architects of St Pancras New Church, the tower of which can be seen to the right, beyond Euston Road. In their early days the Schools provided 20 boys to lead the singing in the Church. The schools remained in use until just after WW II, being closed finally in 1950. The buildings

were not demolished until 1970, when a new square was created on the site. Alongside the school stood St Pancras Church House, a handsome building of 1833 with a tower staircase, designed by William Teulon, brother of the better-known Samuel Sanders Teulon. This was replaced in 1970 by the dark-red-brick **Church House** on the south side of Lancing Street, which incorporates flats and two halls, the lower of which currently houses the Catholic Central Library, whose gilt-lettered gate can be glimpsed behind the Royal George pub. As we shall see later, Roman Catholicism has played a crucial part in the life of Somers Town from its earliest days.

Turn right at the foot of the steps and walk along this west side of Eversholt Street. The **Royal George** opposite was built in 1939 to replace a pub of the same name in Drummond Street. The gold eagles on the corners are the symbol of the brewers Truman, Hanbury & Buxton, whose architect A E Sewell designed this remarkably complete example of a 1930s pub. The interior has fine marquetry panels which contrast the radios and cocktails of the period with the steam age of a century earlier; there is also a large panel depicting the sailing ship after which the pub is named. Beyond the pub is tiny **WELLESLEY PLACE**, all that remains of the little street of the same name (no doubt after the hero of Waterloo – prior to that it had been named Nelson Street after the hero of Trafalgar); in 1901 Wellesley House was built on the site of the street. To the south of this is a derelict site on which stood a seedy terrace that included, on the Grafton Place corner, a chemist's shop. Here once worked Roselie Harris, one of the lady friends of the notorious Rector of Stiffkey, Harold Davidson, known as the Prostitutes' Padre.

Crossing the entrance to the bus station in Euston Square (p 23), note the street opposite, **GRAFTON PLACE,** named after the Duke, and previously known as Seymour Place North. Squares built to attract wealthy residents to a new neighbourhood and the streets immediately leading to them, as Grafton Place does to Euston Square, were usually somewhat more genteel than the back streets. Censuses list, alongside ladies' maids, professors and musicians living in Grafton Place. In 1871 one Henry Edward Leacock listed his occupation as 'Quadrille Harpist' (which to us may sound delightful but could have been nightly drudgery for him). By the 20th century the street had declined, and the artist Geoffrey Fletcher remembered it as a "crumbling relic of a vanished London life. The landlord lived in the basement, the gaslight was always on, the hallways were dark and forbidding to normal people, and smelt of cabbages and cats; the lino was torn and nailed down in a hundred places...". All that remains now is the ghostly outline of

the terraced cottages on the side of the dark tower at the end; the site has been derelict since the mid-20th century.

Nos. 70–71 Euston Square, opposite on the corner with Grafton Place, is the only building still remaining of the original square, and the only one still wholly in residential use. Built in the early 19th century, it has a quite imposing entrance. Originally two private houses, by 1870 these had been joined as a hotel. Maps show it as the 'Clerical Hotel' or the 'Temperance Hotel' – it now remains as a reminder of the myriad hotels of all sizes which once surrounded the station. Subsequently used by the local authority as accommodation for the homeless it had, since 1951, been run as St Philomena's, a hostel for young women students, by the nuns of the Poor Servants of the Mother of God, who later added the substantial extension along Grafton Place. This extension has now been taken over by the Depaul Trust to offer accommodation to the homeless again, the convent still occupying the old part of the building.

The contrast in building materials along this eastern side of the square is telling. St Philomena's is typically Regency, with its combination of London stock brick and stucco (though at one time the front as well as the Grafton Place side was completely stuccoed). The Victorians disapproved of stucco because they felt it masqueraded deceitfully as stone (Dickens referred disparagingly to areas where such

pretensions reigned as 'Stucconia'). The convent's neighbour, built in 1901/2, is an early LCC **fire station**. It uses the provincial red brick much favoured by the Council as we shall see round the corner – bricks whose importation from outside London was made possible by railway transport. The station is a notable Arts and Crafts building, most probably designed by Charles Canning Winmill, head of the section of the LCC Architects' Department devoted to fire stations. Pevsner rated the quirky design one of their most inventive, enjoying its "romantic composition of gables and chimneys". Note the fanciful little balcony at fifth-floor level leading from the upper-floor flat, the quarters of the Divisional Officer North (occupied between 1925 and 1933 by the aptly-named Commander Sir Aylmer Firebrace RN, later Chief Officer of the London Fire Brigade). Below it are gates leading to a now bricked-in archway, the exit for the commander's car; the high round window marks the shaft which housed the connecting lift. Balancing this to the left, the square bay with louvred openings housed the hoist which raised the used hoses to hang up to dry in the days before new materials rendered this unnecessary.

At the traffic lights with **EUSTON ROAD** cross Eversholt Street to the fire station, noting the delicate ornamentation on the Portland stone on its façade. The two large entrances opened from the shed housing the appliances; in 1902 one horse-drawn and one 'steamer'. Sir John Betjeman, on a visit to Euston in 1962 to try to save the Doric arch (p 27), was so impressed with the fire station that he helped it to become Listed Grade II.

There is a history of fire service on the site. An 1867 map marks an 'escape station' here; these were set up by the Royal Society for the Protection of Life from Fire to locate supplementary escapes or ladders. Fire stations (the nearest to this one was at Great Portland Street) were at that date concerned with saving property rather than human lives. Two watchmen were employed to man the ladders and a little box was provided for them to shelter in while on duty. To this day a stint of duty answering 999 calls is known as being 'in the box'.

The fire station was built on the site of Seymour Place, one of the imposing early terraces which had sprung up along the New Road in the 18th century. The fire station's tree-shaded courtyard (the architects carefully included the central plane tree on their plans) gives some idea of how the New Road must have looked. After much discussion in Parliament a rule was imposed that no building was to be allowed within 50 feet of the road. By the end of the century, as shown in Horwood's map of 1799, the road, which still ran mainly through open fields, was here and there lined with terraces with long front gardens – a far cry from today's traffic-choked thoroughfare. A sort of northern by-pass around London, the New Road was intended to allow for much faster transport (for troops as well as animals bound for market) than negotiating 'the stones'. The opportunity for experiments in public transport was seized and London's first omnibus ran from Paddington to the Bank in 1829. One of the early vehicles – Shillibeer's 3-horse bus – can be seen in the London Transport Museum in Covent Garden. A cumbersome wooden box, it has 'Somers Town' among the destinations painted in decorative roundels on its side.

The substantial granite pillar beside the right-hand plane tree is all that remains of the row of pillars which, topped with urns, punctuated the railings in front of the former headquarters of the Hearts of Oak Benefit Society. Formed in 1842 in an upper room of the Bird in Hand tavern in Long Acre, the society had prospered and had built a new grand classical-style headquarters here, opened in 1906 by King Edward VII and Queen Alexandra. Outside was a 7-ft bronze statue of King Edward in full regalia on an 8-ft granite plinth, which was moved to Broadstairs (where it still stands outside a former Hearts of Oak convalescent home) when the building was demolished. The society's old headquarters was replaced by the present 16-storey glass-clad block, now known as **Evergreen House**, opened in 1970.

On Horwood's map of 1799 the area we have just passed was shown as farmland, and Thompson's 1804 map indicates that a large area bounded on the east by Churchway was known as the Lower Brick Field. Horwood's map shows the new development of Somers Town surrounded by such fields, brickmaking being an important activity of local tenant farmers, the Rhodes family (p 63), tenants of the Brill Farm. Brickmaking was an old St Pancras industry creating no pleasant environment: Charles Manby Smith in his 1835 article *How London Grows* complained that "the smell of new-mown hay is superseded by the smell of burning bricks".

The next turning on the left is **CHURCHWAY**, probably the oldest continuously used thoroughfare in Somers Town. While the road appears to take its name from the fact that it leads to St Pancras Church opposite, the name actually predates the 1819 church, probably by some centuries. Originating as a footpath from the south through the pastures of The Brill to Old St Pancras church about 1/2 mile due north (p 100), Churchway's slightly winding route contrasts with the grid pattern of the rest of Somers Town's streets. The little path demarcated the western edge of early Somers Town development – Horwood's map shows its line along the edges of the back gardens of the houses of Chalton Street to the east. But by 1834 it had become a narrow, overcrowded alleyway, one of Somers Town's worst slums, whose entry from Euston Road was, by 1870, via a 'ginnel' only 5 ft wide between the houses. Its entry was not widened until 1906.

Cross to the opposite corner where there still stands, boarded up and seemingly destined for demolition, the former **Elizabeth Garrett Anderson Hospital**. Named after its founder only after her death, it opened as the New Hospital for Women in 1890 (Fig 4). The first of several remarkable women we shall encounter on our explorations of Somers Town, Elizabeth Garrett Anderson (1836–1917) was the first woman in England to qualify in medicine (though she had to go to Paris to do so). She opened her first public dispensary (for women and children only) in Marylebone in 1866 (the date appears on the Euston Road frontage of the hospital), relocating in 1886 to Euston Road, which had the advantage of excellent transport links. The slums of Somers Town offered plenty of work for the doctor, who felt great concern for the health of working-class women. It was the first hospital run for and by women. No male was allowed on the staff – not even a tomcat! One of the country's first women surgeons worked here and one of the hospital's wards was named after her – Louisa Brandreth Aldrich-Blake, whose monument can be seen in nearby Tavistock Square. Dr Anderson was a redoubtable feminist, who at her wedding refused to promise obedience and who wrote that she "married without millinery and almost

without cookery". She joined the suffragettes at the age of 72, and after her retirement from medicine became England's first woman mayor. She would surely be devastated to find her hospital fallen into disuse after barely a century's highly valued service to women.

The hospital, designed by the London Scottish architect John Brydon, provides an interesting contrast to the fire station. The two buildings exemplify two very different strands in Edwardian architecture. The fire station is an outstanding example of Arts and Crafts, inventive and forward-looking, whereas the hospital harks back to the English Baroque in a style disparagingly dubbed 'Wrenaissance'. The hospital partly displaced another of those 18th-century

4   New Hospital for Women (drawing in Building News, May 10 1889)

terraces, Somers Place, a remaining fragment of which can still be seen to the right, behind the Chinese Travel agents beyond the nurses' wing of the hospital opened in 1937. In Somers Place was located another centre of health care for working-class patients: the St Pancras & Northern Dispensary, founded 1810, where Dr Peter Mark Roget, who was much later in his life to publish his famous thesaurus, was one of the very earliest attendant physicians.

At No.1 Somers Place, on the corner of Churchway, lived the painter Thomas Uwins (1782–1857), Royal Academician, Surveyor of Pictures to Queen Victoria and in 1847 appointed Keeper of the National Gallery. A genre painter, best known for once very popular scenes of Italian peasants, he also produced fashion plates for Ackermann as well as writing for the weekly *Repository* under the nom-de-plume "Arbiter Elegantiarum".

Turn left up Churchway and pass the later additions to the hospital, including a prominent Adam-style balcony. At the back, note the gates labelled 'Forty Churchway'; the cobbled slope leads down to the back entrance of the leather works in Chalton Street (p 40). Opposite, left, at the end of Grafton Place, you are confronted by a very forbidding, almost square tower in dark brick, named **Grafton Chambers**. Designed by E Frazer Tomlin in about 1927, its six flats have been home to several

women doctors. The category of name is interesting – 'Chambers' no doubt attempting to attract a professional class of tenant, whereas the red-brick block next to it, designed to house the working classes, still bears its original nameplate "Wellesley Buildings". The last word has long been thought degrading, and the name has been changed to Wellesley *House*. However outdated the nomenclature, the actual nameplate, with its well-designed Arts and Crafts lettering, rather shows up the later plastic signage which surrounds it.

Wellesley House, together with its companion blocks opposite – **Seymour House** and **Winsham House** (originally Somerset, after Lady Henry Somerset, daughter of the 3rd Earl Somers and freeholder of the site, who withdrew her original promise of support for the buildings) – were among the earliest achievements of the London County Council in providing better housing for London's poor. The LCC was empowered by the 1890 Housing of the Working Classes Act to demolish slums and build new houses for rent. Churchway was the first part of Somers Town to be rebuilt; the narrow street, particularly the end away from the Euston Road, was low-lying and damp, and the ill-ventilated houses were home to people from the section of society labelled by Charles Booth as 'very poor, in chronic want'. Between 1899 and 1901, fired with the philanthropic ideals of the

1890s and inspired by the Arts and Crafts movement, the Council's team of architects, led by W E Riley, rebuilt most of Churchway in a way which earned the Pevsner seal of approval: "very pretty for their date and distinguished by their well-proportioned sash windows". Note, behind railings, the wall between Seymour and Winsham Houses; at one time the leather works (p 40) extended this far. Interestingly, above the wall one can see that, unlike Wellesley House, the red brick of the frontages is not continued, the sides and back of the buildings being in stock brick.

Continue along Churchway, past the less distinguished block opposite erected by the LCC in the 1960s, to the junction with **DORIC WAY**, and turn left along it. As its sign tells you, this was originally the eastern end of Drummond Street (p 20). The street was cut in half by the 1960s rebuilding of Euston Station and this portion was then renamed after the Doric arch that graced the Drummond Street entrance to the old station (p 27). A dairy once occupied the triangular site bounded by Doric Way, Drummond Crescent and Crace Street. The whole site is now taken up by the first blocks of flats built by the St Pancras Housing Association (SPHA), formed in 1924 as the St Pancras House Improvement Society by the charismatic Anglo-Catholic priest Basil Jellicoe (1899–1935).

Despite his untimely death nearly 70 years ago Father Jellicoe (Fig. 5), who was sent to Somers Town as a missionary from Magdalen College, Oxford, is still remembered with great affection by long-term Somers Town residents. The Society's original intention of buying up and converting existing properties was thwarted by the poor condition of the slum dwellings, and by the impossible task of eliminating the bedbugs and other wildlife with which they were infested. Ian Hamilton, the architect of the new flats, took great pains to discourage these vermin by choosing special materials and by painting rather than papering the walls. The first flats were occupied in 1928, at affordable rents ranging from 9s. to 22s.6d. per week (45p – £1.25). The architect shared with Father Jellicoe a belief in the value of art for everyone and they commissioned the versatile Gilbert Bayes (perhaps best known for the *Queen of Time* figure holding aloft the clock above Selfridge's main Oxford Street entrance) to provide decorative elements for the flats. The subjects chosen also point to the religious impulse behind the buildings. On two balconies of **St Anne's Flats**, the block facing you, are reliefs of eagles with a fish – both Christian symbols. The inner courtyard was furnished with a ring of drying posts topped with ceramic doves surrounding a central post whose finial is a model of a carpenter's bag of tools (alluding to St Joseph – the three blocks are named after the Holy Family). The current finials are replacements, the originals having

disappeared only to turn up later at a fine art auction! A closer view of these finials is available at the very attractive small display entitled 'Housing is Not Enough' at the British Library (which we will visit later).

5   Father Basil Jellicoe with coalman Mr Tattershall (photograph c.1926–9)

The buildings demolished to make way for the new flats housed many small

businesses, and St Anne's incorporated several shops; the semi-basement flats still have their big shop windows. The corner flat decorated with seafood tiles was a fish shop, rehousing the fishmonger whose previous shop stood on the site. Beyond is **St Mary's Flats**, where iconoclasts have been at work – a sad statue of the Virgin holds a now headless baby – and just visible further along its façade is a Della Robbia style relief. To the left and slightly below street level is gated **CRACE STREET**. This was originally known as Little Drummond Street and was renamed after J G Crace (1809–89), a leading furniture maker and decorator, who worked on the Houses of Parliament and, in 1866, designed the ornamentation of new St Pancras Church. Crace Street houses the 1955 **Edith Neville Cottages** with their rose-filled front gardens. The cottages commemorate another stalwart of the SPHA, the councillor Edith Neville (see p 49) who died in 1951. One of the cottages was the gift of the Brewers' Company as a tribute to Miss Neville's concern for pubs; she shared with Father Jellicoe a belief in the great importance of the pub to the community, especially in poor areas (p 55). Beside the entrance is **Ian Hamilton House**, named after the SPHA's architect who died in 1971. (For the full story of the SPHA, since 2000 the St Pancras and Humanist Housing Association, see *Housing is not enough* by Malcolm Holmes).

Turn right into Eversholt Street, past an early-19th-century brick terrace with prominent relieving arches to the first floor windows, to the corner of Drummond Crescent. The site behind the Seven 'O' fish and chip shop at one time housed the offices of the SPHA. Continue past Art Deco **Regent House**. Behind this is a Catholic enclave including, as it has done since the early days of Somers Town, church, convent and schools, all largely the creation of another charismatic priest, the Abbé Carron, whose house is shown in Fig 6. Before turning our attention to the church note the little sandwich bar at **No. 74**. This belongs to the St Aloysius church and was once run as the One World Shop, selling Traidcraft goods. The shop was set up by Bruce Kent, priest at St Aloysius from 1977 until 1980, when he was released to work full-time for CND.

Past the **Prince Arthur** pub, and on the corner of Phoenix Road (p 38), is the Catholic church of **St Aloysius**, its west wall carrying a figure of the Risen Christ by D J Purness. The present church was built in 1966–8, its architect A J Newton creating a bold juxtaposition of straight and curved elements with notable stained glass by the Whitefriars studio. Inside is a plaque commemorating the laying of the foundation stone in 1967 by Cardinal Heenan and a 'history corner', which among other items of interest includes a bust of the Abbé Carron, "friend of the destitute and

unfortunate, comforter of the afflicted"; also a cutting from the *Penny Illustrated* for 6 October 1888 with a large engraving showing the parish priest of the time in front of the altar, fighting off an evil-looking gang – "London's Reign of Terror: Burglars find their match in Father Ryan at St Aloysius Church". Nowadays such incidents mean that the church is kept locked; however, access is possible through the sandwich bar.

Pause at the church to consider the history of the area. The early development of Somers Town was badly affected by lack of funds during the Napoleonic wars. What had been planned as a relatively genteel neighbourhood (although the houses were for the most part only 3rd or 4th rate) soon found itself, as Dickens put it, "come down in the world and taken to letting lodgings". Among those who took advantage of the cheap accommodation were many émigrés from the French Revolution, including a large contingent of clergymen, banished in 1792 for their refusal to take the oath of allegiance to the French State. In 1799, coming via Jersey and Fitzroy Square, there arrived in Somers Town the wonderfully named Guy Toussaint Julien Carron de la Carrière (1760–1821). The Abbé Carron brought with him the school he had set up earlier in Fitzrovia and expanded his activities in Somers Town, eventually setting up two hospitals, a seminary and a church, as well as a range of schools for boys and girls, rich and poor. The

missionary fervour of the Catholic émigré priests was commented on by Prime Minister Pitt the Younger. Carron "had a spiritual audacity that seemed to conjure chapels, schools, hospitals and libraries from the very lap of the angels"; the comparison with Basil Jellicoe is interesting.

Following the 1791 Toleration Act Roman Catholic churches were no longer illegal but were still required to be sited in quiet streets, away from any main thoroughfare. Abbé Carron's church of St Aloysius (known to its French congregation as St Louis de Gonzague) was built in 1808 facing the Polygon (p 51), on the site now occupied by the convent of St Aloysius a few hundred yards along Phoenix Road. The little church, which had a classical, stuccoed façade (added in 1830) and an elaborately decorated interior, was to play a very important part in the Catholic Revival in Britain. In September 1889 a Requiem mass was held there for Pascal Paoli, the exiled Corsican patriot who had died in London in 1807 and was buried in Old St Pancras churchyard. Baroness Burdett-Coutts obtained permission for the exhumation and sent Paoli's body home on her private yacht for reburial on his native island. The little church was badly bombed in WW II and not saved.

In addition to the numerous clergymen many poorer French émigrés found lodgings in Somers Town. These included servants of wealthier émigrés who had settled in the neighbouring parish of St Marylebone and poorer aristocrats, such as Charles and Louise-Julie Dufayis, whose daughter Caroline was baptised in St Pancras Old Church on 1 January 1794. After the death of Charles, mother and daughter survived on a monthly allowance of £2 13s 6d [£2.68] plus a further £1 for an English maid (as Mme Dufayis was in poor health). In 1800 Napoleon issued an edict allowing émigrés to return, and the six-year-old Caroline travelled to Paris with her mother. She later married François Baudelaire; their son Charles, poet of *Les Fleurs du Mal*, was born in 1821. Another notable child of émigrés was Francis Gasquet, born in Somers Town in 1846, who in 1914 became one of Britain's few churchmen to be elevated to the rank of Cardinal. Another émigré (though to Hamburg rather than London) was the Abbé Jacques Delille, known as the poet of the emigration; his 1838 poem *Malheur et Pitié* includes the line "Salut, ô Sommerstown, abri cher à la France". It seems that Somers Town was better known abroad than in the UK; refugees from the oppressive regime in Spain also found lodgings in the area from around 1823. They too were given an allowance and, despite finding Somers Town cold and inhospitable, Alcala Galiano, former member of the Spanish Cortes and later to become Professor of Spanish at University College, London, wrote that Somers Town was known in his native land as "a miniature constitutional Spain which made room for a great number of homeless Spaniards" (for further details on the Spanish community in Somers Town see *Camden History Review* 6).

6 Abbé Carron's house, Evesham Buildings, formerly occupied by Jacob Leroux, the developer of Somers Town (drawing, 1859)

This end of **PHOENIX ROAD**, between Eversholt Street and the open square, was originally called Charles Street. Here lived Henry Croft (1862–1930), the original Pearly King. His funeral was attended by 100 Pearly Kings and Queens and the cortège, as it made its way from Charles Street to St Pancras Cemetery (Finchley), was watched by a crowd of thousands. A statue of the costermongers' hero, clad in one of his famous Pearly suits, can be seen on his tomb.

Moving along Phoenix Road on this south side, past the church's Primary School (the date of 1852 on the wall commemorates a rebuilding of the school), the 1960s building at **No.32** is the new convent. The letters "FCJ" on its door stand for the Faithful Companions of Jesus, the order founded by a refugee from the 1830 revolution in France, Madame Marie Madeleine Victoire de Bonnault d'Houet. She also founded the convent school, previously the girls' department of St Aloysius School, which survives next door as **Maria Fidelis**. Its present name appears on the elaborately decorated doorway of **No.34** with its terracotta foliate heads and above the door a heart pierced by arrows (perhaps the doorway of the original convent building?).

Continue, past an alleyway (to which we shall shortly return), to the corner with Chalton Street. Here at No.42 is the **Hopscotch Asian Women's Centre** –

evidence of the continuing cosmopolitan nature of the area. The name comes from a club founded by the Save the Children Fund in 1943 to offer activities for orphaned and homeless children. In 1982 the club's building in Eversholt Street (leased from the SPHA) as well as the name was taken over to offer training, education and advice for immigrant Asian families, moving here in 1994. The building, with its pleasant oriel windows, had previously housed the Margaret Club and Day Nursery, which opened here in 1931.

On this corner (Fig 6) stood Evesham Buildings, where William Godwin lived in 1797 before moving to the Polygon on his marriage to Mary Wollstonecraft. Also here lived the Abbé Carron and before that Jacob Leroux, magistrate for Middlesex and the original developer of Somers Town. For a short period around 1798 a barracks of the Life Guards stood behind the buildings – the riotous behaviour of some Irish recruits led to their committal to the House of Correction by Mr Justice Leroux.

Retrace your steps and turn left down the little alleyway rather grandly named **CLARENDON GROVE** (as it ran out of Clarendon Square, p 51). There is not much to be seen along here, but it was once lined with houses and workshops, several of them involved in piano making, an important industry in the area. London, following the impetus of J C ('English') Bach (p 99), played a crucial role in the

early development of the piano; many young people in Somers Town were apprenticed to workshops making pianos or piano components. The area around Drummond Street and Drummond Crescent housed many such workshops as late as the 1920s. Between 1890 and 1927 the Crescent was also home to one Henry Starck, who claimed to be the only bagpipe maker south of the Border.

The alley leads us back to the junction of Churchway and **DRUMMOND CRESCENT** where we are once more on the boundary of the Somers estate. Opposite, outside the former Lion & Lamb pub (there are current plans to build a block of flats on the site), is a bollard with the crest of George IV (which has probably, however, migrated here from the Crown-owned Regent's Park area).

Look right, along the crescent: at the front of **St Joseph's Flats** the sign with a red cross marks the entrance to **Basil Jellicoe Hall**, built in 1936 as a memorial to the young priest who had done so much to change the face of Somers Town. Refurbished in 1991, together with the surrounding blocks, the hall serves as the venue for many community functions, as Father Jellicoe would have wished. The opposite curve of the little crescent has, since 1984, been taken up by a Metropolitan Police garage; before that the building, dating from the 1930s, housed a variety of establishments serving the motor trade, and more recently served as a garage for Evening Standard vans.

Look to your left noting, opposite the former pub, a little terrace in Victorian Gothic style – one of the mosaic panels over the windows shows its date as 1882. Turn left into the alleyway which is the continuation of **CHURCHWAY** and the first part of the road to be built up. Despite the 1990s SPHA flats on the corner, the narrow alley retains a flavour of its 19th-century origin, with a drain down its centre and a pair of former gas lampposts. Among the anonymous small businesses here, one proclaims itself clearly: the black door of the red-painted **No.70** bears a label 'Mick's Eel Supply'. Previously a fishmongers (and possibly earlier still a cats' meat dealer) it was taken over by Micky Jenrick whose chief interest was eel processing: "what I don't know about eels there ain't to know". He and his workers, with ankle-length aprons flapping round their big rubber boots, wheeling great baskets of eels and whelks, brought much life to the alley until the 1980s, but sadly the trade is now in decline and, although he retains the premises, Micky now only deals out of Billingsgate Market. On the far left-hand corner of the alley stood an early branch of Sainsbury's (Fig 7). It was opened in 1889 on the site of a dairy owned by Ben Staples, whose daughter Mary Ann married John James Sainsbury, founder of the firm.

We now come out into **CHALTON**

STREET (the origin of the name seems lost; a 1797 map shows it as Charlton Street), the southern part of which is described here, the northern part in Route 4 (p 64). For the past three-quarters of a century it has been the heart of Somers Town, its main shopping street and once one of the busiest market streets in London, where just about anything could be bought. Chalton Street was almost a village

7   Sainsbury's, Nos. 86-87 Chalton Street (photo, 1904)

community in itself, boasting residents such as the eccentric 18th-century physician Dr Squirrell, author (1798) of *Maxims of Health or an Essay on Indigestion… Also Remarks on Sea Bathing* (a copy can be consulted in the Wellcome Library). The Doctor was also resident apothecary to the Smallpox and Inoculation Hospital (p 75). He was rudely, but no doubt aptly, nicknamed by the locals 'Dr. Squirt'.

A handbill announced the reopening on 7 July 1823 at (then) No.57 Chalton Street of 'The Original Sommers Town Academy'. Young Gentlemen could be "accurately instructed in Greek, Latin, French, English, Geography with the use of Globes, Astronomy, Drawing, Mathematics and other Branches of useful and polite Literature in a lofty, commodious and well-ventilated room". According to the proprietor, Mr Samuel Maynard, the academy was "calculated to relieve the incapacity of the Dull, not less than to give full effect to the innate gifts of Genius".

Nowadays, the market still operates, but only on Friday mornings, selling cheap clothing. Before 1930 the main market was in Chapel Street, which no longer exists but then ran opposite through to what is now Midland Road. Alongside Chapel Street stood the girls' school of Christ Church; the playground to the left marks the site of the actual church. Together with its schools this was built in 1868, paid for by the philanthropist George Moore, to replace

St Luke's church (p 104), which had been demolished to make way for St Pancras Station. A large barn-like neo-Gothic building (seating 1200) with a steeple, Christ Church, was destroyed by bombing in 1941.

Opposite us stands the **Somers Town Coffee House**, whose name harks back to its 18th-century ancestor. The original coffee house was much frequented by the foreigners of Somers Town, and was noted for serving French coffee in the best Parisian style. It also offered the pleasures of a tea garden and skittle ground, and was a posting house. The original building stood further south, the present building dating from 1927–8, when it was incorporated into the LCC development which occupies most of the eastern side of this part of Chalton Street.

Cross the street, turn right and look south along the western side of the street, which preserves buildings from the early days of Somers Town. A few late Victorian buildings stand out from the range, notably **No.57** with its banded brickwork and mosaic panels above the tall first-floor windows; it bears a strong resemblance to the terrace round the corner in Churchway. **No.49** until 2001 housed the Pensioners' Centre, home to two campaigning organisations and named **Jack Jones House** after the one-time leader of the T&G union and fighter for pensioners' rights. The imposing pair of yellow-brick

buildings at **Nos.39–41** was built in 1884 as the headquarters of Connolly's, suppliers of leather to the motor industry, most prestigiously to Rolls Royce. Connolly's leather can also be found in the Houses of Parliament, on Concorde and in the new British Library. From humble beginnings as boot repairers in Euston Road, the brothers John Joseph and Frederick Connolly so prospered that eventually 10,000 hides a day were processed in their works near Wimbledon. Big trolleys piled high with them were a familiar sight in Chalton Street until 1980 when the firm moved, ending up in Ashford in Kent. **No.39** (Unity House), with the prominent hoist, now houses the National Union of Rail Maritime and Transport Workers, displaced from the Euston Road by the Wellcome Trust (p 22). The pub next door, commemorating Queen Victoria, has been closed for many years.

Chalton Street has a prestigious new neighbour – the British Library – whose architect Colin St John Wilson predicted in 1998 that "'a whole new sector of London life is about to be generated". The tide of plate glass creeping along Chalton Street seems to prove him right. The French community has long gone, but the street retains Somers Town's cosmopolitan character, with a Filipino Centre, two establishments entitled Dar Al-Hekma (House of Wisdom), a centre for Bahrainis, a Halal shop, a sari shop and a Brazilian restaurant.

Continue south towards Euston Road. A little farther on, between two eating-places at Nos.11&15, is a metal gate across the entrance to **CHRISTOPHER PLACE,** a pleasant cobbled yard. Probably named after Christopher Kite, whose ventilating, sanitary and heating works were situated nearby on Euston Road, the yard as recently as 1980 contained a working blacksmith. Now it is home to one of Somers Town's most pleasing and least dominant pieces of modern architecture, the pioneering **Speech, Language and Hearing Centre**. Designed by Troughton McAslan, it opened in 1995. The only one of its kind in the UK, the centre provides teaching and therapy for 60 children under 5 with hearing impairment or delay in developing speech, language and communication.

The pub named **The Rocket** is part of a chain known as 'It's a Scream' and consequently flaunts a crude version of the famous painting which Edvard Munch completed in 1893. The pub's original name, The Rising Sun, is still there in the decorative red brickwork, as is the image of a rising sun, together with the date of the rebuilding of the pub by Shoebridge and Rising in 1899. The building stands well back from the Euston Road in keeping with the original 50-ft rule; a pub has stood on this corner since the early days of Somers Town, when it would have had a view across the New Road towards open fields.

John Thompson's map of 1804 vividly evokes the scene, even drawing in the five-barred gates into those fields. According to the memoir of Thomas Uwins written by his widow Sarah (herself born and brought up in Somers Town), "the fields were so dangerous after dark that…the inhabitants of Somers Town used to pay a man to blow a horn every half hour, near the Rising Sun public house at the corner of Chalton Street and the New Road; at which signal those who wished to cross over would assemble and proceed in a body for mutual protection".

Across Chalton Street the tower block, which surmounted the former St Pancras Library (see below), was first occupied by British Petroleum and latterly housed an advertising agency and documentary filming company before being converted to a hotel. Behind the block is an ostensibly anonymous roadway known as **WEIR'S PASSAGE**, seemingly after Alexander Weir, landlord of a tavern on the New Road about 1800. There is nothing much to be seen here now, no hint of the crowded scene described by one former resident born in the West London Mission Hall which stood on the corner. As late as the 1920s he wrote "it was an alley festering on both sides with filthy hovels where no policeman would venture, although the sisters attached to the Mission were allowed to come and go unmolested" (Fig 8, p 42). The Mission occupied the People's Hall, a castellated

building erected by Lady Somerset and leased to the Methodists in 1892. The building was also an early home for the St Pancras School for Mothers founded in 1907, and later removed to Ampthill Square (p 63). In a borough in which 1,000 babies a year died before their first birthday, it offered cheap, or even free, meals for expectant or nursing mothers and gave classes in infant care. Cookery lessons were even available at home, given by an instructress who came to be affectionately known as 'The Pudding Lady'.

To the left of Weir's Passage is **Levita House**, largest of the blocks of flats put up as part of the LCC's extensive slum clearance scheme of the 1920s and 30s. The Ossulston Estate, of which Levita House is the largest block, is the most important inner-city estate of the inter-war period. The LCC architect G Topham Forrest had visited Vienna and his general layout and severity of ornament owe much to the grand housing schemes for workers' flats in that city; the steeply pitched pantiled roofs give the blocks a distinctively Continental feel. Six of the row of lock-up shops which front the block were taken by Sainsbury's in 1953 when they had outgrown their original shop on the corner of Churchway. The unusual name derives from Sir Cecil Bingham Levita (1867–1953), who was Chairman of the LCC in 1928–9.

Turn right through the first big archway into the courtyard, where dusty hawthorns

MISSION

MEN'S
INSTITUTE

CHALTON STREET N.W.I

S. HAIRCUTT

SHA

SHAVING
SHAVING

PARRY'S
SHAVING
SALOON.

are all that remain of the original garden. Exiting by the opposite archway, cross Ossulston Street (p 44), and turning right, walk south towards the traffic lights at **EUSTON ROAD**.

On the corner, at **No.100**, are the main doors to the **Shaw Park Plaza Hotel**, the lowest four storeys of which formerly housed St Pancras Library. Designed by Elidir Davies, it was opened in 1971 by Princess Anne and included a major reference library, but was closed only 20 years later by a cash-strapped Camden Council. To the right is the entrance to the refurbished **Shaw Theatre**, once home to the National Youth Theatre and main venue for Camden's lively Arts Festival. Outside the theatre entrance (erected over the demolished Eliza Doolittle pub) is a large sculpture entitled *St Joan* that used to stand outside the library entrance. An abstract construction by Keith Grant (better known as a painter), it was initially seen as a symbol of socialism. The saint's armour is suggested by steel panels, perforated by rods which represent the lances of the warring French and English.

Turn briefly left along Euston Road, then left again through a portico, with iron gates designed by the renowned lettering

8 Weir's Passage in the 1920s

artist David Kindersley. Facing you is an example of English Free Style architecture, the **British Library**. Built on the site of the Midland Railway's former goods depot, the library was opened by the Queen in 1998. It was designed by Professor Sir Colin St John Wilson, with brick and slate chosen to harmonise with its neighbour the former Midland Grand Hotel. Its construction produced vast quantities of waste that were used to create, among other facilities, a ski slope at Beckton in East London.

The British Library site once lay partly on the Skinners' estate (p 11). West Street, running diagonally across what is now the library forecourt, formed the Somers–Skinners boundary. Along the New Road fronting the library site stood a terrace named Judd Place West; at No.16 of which in 1796 lived Mary Wollstonecraft, then carrying on a premarital affair with William Godwin, at that time living at No.25 Chalton Street. Behind this the 14-acre site was a maze of streets with little courts and alleys crammed into every available nook and cranny between and behind earlier buildings.

In 1874 the Midland Railway acquired the site for its new Somers Town Goods Depot, and an estimated 10,000 people were displaced, their houses being cleared by 1878, though work did not begin on the goods yard until 1883, and its magnificent, red-brick Gothic arcaded walls were finished only in 1887. The clearance caused further overcrowding in the adjacent, already teeming, areas but the railway company failed to do anything about this, or even to estimate the scale of the problem. To make matters worse the railway company was applauded for doing away with the old slums; an article in *The Builder* said "a more dilapidated or disease-ridden block of hovels does not exist in any part of the metropolis". It was not until 1894 that the railway company erected blocks of flats on the site of the old Polygon (p 53) to help ease the overcrowding, and then mainly to house railway workers.

The railway goods depot was built on two levels, the lines being raised to cross Pancras Road and, eventually, the canal to the north. Innovative hydraulic lifts operated on this site to raise and lower coal, milk, fish, potatoes and other miscellaneous freight for which the railway goods depot was used between 1887 and 1968.

Today, the library's spacious piazza where one may sit and enjoy a coffee or, in summer, a variety of performances, is dominated by Eduardo Paolozzi's huge bronze of Isaac Newton, inspired by the image by William Blake (and paid for by the football pools!). To the right, the architect has designed the outline of the library's conference centre so as to frame a cluster of towers of the St Pancras Midland Hotel.

The library has the deepest basement in London, which houses 300km of shelving for 12 million books assembled from 18 different buildings. The exhibition galleries, displaying such treasures as Magna Carta and the Lindisfarne Gospels, are open to all. Inside you will find a café, from which one can contemplate the new home created for the King's Library, previously housed in the British Museum. The 65,000 volumes, collected by George III and given to the nation by George IV, are now contained in a 6-storey glass and bronze tower with their spines facing outwards, their bindings forming a rich tapestry of subtle leathers and gold tooling. The books are actually available to readers, mobile shelving and internal lifts facilitating their retrieval by staff. At the back of the basement is a small exhibition about the SPHA, with three sculptures by Gilbert Bayes.

Return to the piazza and if you wish to continue with Route 3 take the exit into Ossulston Street. If not, go past the Conference Centre on your left. The exit beyond leads to Euston Road 100 yards from King's Cross main line and Underground stations and a number of bus stops.

Route 3
Somers Town (north & east)

Our second Somers Town walk begins more or less where the first one ended, at the British Library on Euston Road, midway between Euston and King's Cross. If continuing from Route 2, leave the library piazza at its southwest corner, adjacent to the Shaw Park Plaza Hotel.

Walk north along **OSSULSTON STREET**, passing on your left the east side of **Levita House** (see also p 41). This section of the building now belongs to the SPHA and has been recently redecorated. Colin St John Wilson, the British Library's architect, was very complimentary about the design of these flats. Further on, past the back of the library, the view opens up to the right to reveal the imposing train shed of St Pancras station.

Roughly level with the second arched entry to Levita House was a junction with Chapel Street, the forerunner of Chalton Street as the main market street of Somers Town. On one corner, at No.69, stood an exotically named pub, the African Chief. On the southeast corner was the place of worship to which Chapel Street, and

Chapel Path before it, owed their names. Originally Anglican, it had adjoined an obscure burial ground known to have been functioning 'behind Somers Place' in 1798. From 1802, two quite distinct Baptist congregations successively occupied the building. The first of these remained for half a century, naming it Beulah Chapel, rebuilding it in 1821 after a fire, and opening there a 'Lancasterian' school, before departing in 1852 for the new Zion Chapel in Goldington Crescent (p 66). A second flock of Baptists then moved into the Chapel Street building, which became their Bethel Chapel; they stayed only briefly, leaving again in 1856. The premises were then reclaimed by the Anglicans, serving as the mission hall of nearby Christ Church (p 40), and also housing the Agar Town Ragged School, displaced from its home ground by the Midland Railway.

The southern end of Ossulston Street was at first known as Wilsted Street. The stretch ahead has borne the Ossulston name since the earliest days of Somers Town, when it was known as Ossulston Buildings. The name was borrowed from one of the 'hundreds' of Middlesex, whose meeting place was by Oswulf's Stone (at what is now Marble Arch), and of which St Pancras parish was a part.

Continue northward, passing modern **Hadstock House**, built on an open space once occupied by Eastnor Place and the Christ Church National School for Boys.

Chamberlain House, beyond, was the first block to be erected on the LCC's Ossulston Estate. At the north end of the building is a foundation stone laid in 1928 by Neville Chamberlain, then Minister for Health. The building fell prey to a serious fire in May 1985, when 27 flats were destroyed.

Opposite, in early 2002, there still stands a remnant of the 3/4mile-long 1887 arcaded wall which once surrounded the MR goods depot. Singled out by Pevsner for its excellent detailing, the brickwork is much admired for its craftsmanship, the evenness of laying and delicacy of pointing. The railway companies generally did much to improve the standard of bricklaying. The unusually small bricks were imported from Leicestershire and the whole yard was lined with blue bricks from Staffordshire, which offered excellent damp-proofing. The Euston Road frontage was treated more decoratively with stone dressings to the brickwork, delicately hammered iron grilles and impressive wrought iron gates – a pair of these can be seen at the entrance to the Camley Street Natural Park (p 91).

As you turn right into **BRILL PLACE**, the blue facing of the interior can be seen through the gateway. On the north side of the street is **Phoenix Court**, a post-WW II block of offices and 'luxury flats' taken over by Camden Council in 1967, where we should pause. There is no street sign on this corner except a notice stating "Formerly Phoenix Road". Brill Place was, until quite recently, part of Phoenix Road (p 38), known until 1937 as Phoenix Street. Bebbington suggests that the name derived from a local tavern; if it ever existed, it must have been short-lived. It would be pleasing to imagine the street as having risen phoenix-like from the ashes (or dust-heaps) which once abounded locally.

The new name of the street was suggested by the Borough Archivist, Malcolm Holmes. We are here close to the site of the Brill farmhouse (Fig 9). The Brill name takes us further back in history than we have yet been, though not quite as far as imagined by Dr William Stukeley, the 18th-century antiquarian "living in the half-visionary world of the past". According to him, the name indicated that near here lay the site of one of Julius Caesar's encampments; the same claim has been made for other similarly named places, including one in Holland, but modern research disputes these claims. The name is now taken to be from the old French word for a park or wood stocked with beasts of the chase. It survives here as a reminder of the time when the area was open country. A comfortable rural tavern called The Brill was recorded as early as 1690. The pond outside was apparently much favoured by 18th-century would-be suicides. The publisher and bookseller, Samuel Bagster, wrote of his visit as a child, in about 1780, to his uncle

who lived in a hamlet called the Brill. The uncle ran a brick, tile and chimney-pot factory, which no doubt later supplied materials for the new Somers Town which was soon to overrun the rural scene.

The street pattern hereabouts changed radically after the arrival of the Midland Railway. Middlesex Street, which once crossed Phoenix Street here, was home to colonies of costermongers and of

9 Brill Farmhouse (drawing, c.1800?)

woodcutters, both male and female. It was noted for its 'marine stores', shops selling very cheap goods; one Victorian observer remarked that their presence was "suggestive not so much of thrift as of extreme poverty". Middlesex Street vanished in the 1890s, to be replaced by Purchese Street (p 48), which shortly comes in from the left. Beyond it lies the site of the Midland Railway's Purchese Street Coal Depot. Opened in 1898, it covered 7 acres and, like the neighbouring goods depot, was on two levels. Closed in 1968, the coal depot was demolished, and its site was redeveloped by Camden Council a decade later. Two acres became the leafy **Purchese Street Open Space**, sometimes known as 'Somers Green'. Before us, at the southwest corner of the park, a fragment of the depot's red-brick outer wall survives.

Continue along Brill Place. Again there are interesting views of the back of the British Library flanked by the huge train shed of St Pancras. The northern half of the goods depot site is (in 2002) vacant – the British Library project ran out of cash, only a third of the planned scheme being built – and currently accommodates a large conglomeration of portacabins housing offices for the Channel Tunnel Rail Link which is due to have its terminal at St Pancras by 2007; halfway along Brill Place is the **Visitor Centre** for the new terminal, open on weekdays.

Crossing the site of the Open Space, from north to south, was once the Brill Path, an ancient footway forming the eastern boundary of Lord Somers' estate; by 1834, this had been developed as Brill Terrace. Mostly residential, with a sprinkling of corner shops, it was later renamed Brill Street, before finally adopting the name of Goldington Street, its northerly continuation. Straddling its junction with what is now Brill Place was an east-facing Brill Crescent, with its own pub, the Bee Hive. Both Crescent and Street were demolished to make way for the coal depot, and replaced by the new Purchese Street on a more westerly alignment.

On the site to your right, Brill Street continued south, as Brill Row, into the bustling Brill Market. Bagster's 'hamlet' had by then been engulfed by densely packed housing, but its tavern survived, rebuilt as 'Brill House' by a wealthy brickmaker called Benjamin Perry (cf. Perry Street, p 88). The new pub became the focus for a boisterous market and costermongers' colony. The market flourished, attracting customers from miles around to the lively scene of cheap stalls (Fig 10). It was a popular venue for the soap-box clergy: a handbill of 1856 announced that Mr James Dupe, "the converted poacher", was to preach at the Brill on 10 December – "Working men come as you are and hear the Gospel from one of yourselves". The market eventually

became so raucous ("a scene of great excitement on Saturday nights and Sunday mornings") that it was suppressed as a nuisance in 1858. The tavern was demolished in 1865, another casualty of the railway company.

Pass Cooper's Lane on the left and walk on to the junction of Brill Place with Midland Road (p 103), On the right-hand corner, where Phoenix Street once met Brewer Street, was a little street known as Garden Gate; there stood one of the predecessors of St Aloysius Church, a little Catholic chapel founded by Abbé Luc Chantrel and known delightfully as 'Our Lady of the Garden Gate'. Today a little building with a tall chimney (marked on a 1950s plan as a mess room) can be seen above the old goods depot wall. This marks the spot where railway tracks once crossed on a bridge (demolished in the 1980s) to take goods trains into the upper level of the depot. If you examine the wall below, behind an advertising hoarding, you can see that a stretch of brickwork does not match, the bricks here being larger and slightly different in colour. The same bridge across Pancras Road carried coal trains into the Purchese Street coal depot and to a set of 11 elevated sidings at its south end, whence wagons were conveyed to their final resting-place by a complex system of traversers.

Ahead, we are confronted with a glimpse of the huge works underway for the Channel Tunnel Rail Link, yet another

10   Brill House & Market on a Sunday morning (drawing, ?1850s). To the right ,Weston Street (see p 88) wrongly labelled by the artist.

phase of disruption for local residents. We turn northwest, however, through a part of 'Somers Town' which was, historically, not Somers Town at all, lying as it did on the always more respectable Brewers' estate. In 1575, a benevolent London brewer called Richard Platt gave land he owned locally to endow the public school at Aldenham (Herts.), his birthplace. Described as "all those 3 pastures of ground lying nighe the Churche of St. Pancrasse…containing an estimacion of 20 acres, more or less", the property was vested in the Brewers' Company as trustees. Its southeast corner, on the site of St Pancras Station, was the earliest to be developed for housing, from 1811.

The eastern extremity of Brill Place began as Elstree Street, a cul-de-sac off Old St Pancras Road; the livery company was at first reluctant to link it with the troubled Somers Town development to the west. By 1834, Stanmore Street and Watford Street had been built on the 'Brewers' Field' to the north of where you stand. These were later demolished for the building of the Purchese Street coal depot. After its closure in 1968, the latter was in turn pulled down. The east side of its site became Camden Council's **Coopers Lane Estate**. High-rise housing was by then out of favour; the intention here was to create a more traditional street environment. The 'Coopers' name may well commemorate a long demolished Coopers' Arms pub;

located in nearby former Hampden Street, it was licensed as a theatre in 1861–2.

Retrace your steps to **COOPERS LANE** and turn north along it. This is the estate's mostly pedestrian spinal route, lined by houses and blocks of maisonettes in brown brick. The Lane has a tranquil, 'suburban' feel; much of the coal depot's Pancras Road frontage was retained (out of sight to your right), partly as a buffer against noise from the road and railway. Also behind the houses on your right is the estate's vehicular access road, known officially as **NEVILLE CLOSE**, after SPHA stalwart Edith Neville. At a crossing of paths, turn left to leave the estate through (unlabelled) **HAMPDEN CLOSE**, whose name derives from that of former Hampden Street (p 50). On the north side is **Clyde Court**, 46 units of sheltered housing for the elderly. The block's name recalls another lost pub, the Lord Clyde, which once stood nearby at No.29 Phoenix Street, and whose sign in turn honoured a veteran of the Crimean War.

Still cobbled **PURCHESE STREET**, into which we emerge up the ramp, dates only from 1895, shortly before the building of the coal depot. Frederick Purchese, of Ossulston Street (and later of Platt Street), was a St Pancras Churchwarden at the time; in 1900 he became the LCC member for St Pancras East. Turn right along Purchese Street, passing on your left the rear of the Edith Neville school (p 49).

The modern council flats at **Nos.9–15**, to which we cross, are in stock brick and classically proportioned, harmonising with the 19th-century houses in Goldington Street beyond.

Turn left at **PLATT STREET**, which owes its name to the philanthropic brewer Richard Platt (see above). The street once continued east to meet Pancras Road, but after WW II surrendered its eastern end to the grounds of The Chenies (p 68). This part of the Brewers' estate was developed in 1849–54. Original houses on the south side of the street have given way to the low-rise 1970s council flats of **Somers Close**, which covers the site of the old local police station, a scrap-yard and, on the southeast corner, the British Transport Commission's post-WW II 'St Pancras School for Apprentices'. Surviving opposite are two ranges of renovated 3-storey houses with stuccoed rusticated ground-floor walls, and round-arched doorways with keystones, all as specified by the Brewers' Company in its building leases. Behind them are secluded communal gardens, carved out of the original back gardens of houses in intersecting streets when the neighbourhood, bomb-damaged in WW II, was 'rehabilitated' by Camden Council c.1972.

Halfway along, cross the street and turn right into **PENRYN STREET**. Originally Percy Street, this was renamed by the Metropolitan Board of Works in 1865 as part of a major exercise to eliminate

London's many street-name duplications. Some of the new names were quite arbitrary: here, at least the first two letters were the same. Penryn Street is delightfully intact, comprising two complete terraces of partly stuccoed houses, all retaining their original ornamented cast-iron balconies. The four corner houses in this symmetrically built street have porticoes.

MEDBURN STREET, which we meet at a T-junction, derives its name from a Medburn Farm at Aldenham. Dating again from 1849–54, its houses were converted into flats and maisonettes as part of Camden's c.1972 rehabilitation. Most still have their original decorative balconies, which are continuous on the south side; all are Grade II Listed.

Turn left and pause at the junction, noting on the north corner an old metal street sign marked "Medburn Street NW". We are at the junction with **CHARRINGTON STREET**, its name borrowed from the well-known brewing company (eventually merged with Bass), which confirms that we are still on the old Brewers' estate. Directly opposite there once stood the Brewers' Hall public house, host in 1881 to the Social Revolutionary & Anarchist Conference. No houses at all survive on the street's west side, now lined wholly by the precincts of **South Camden Community School**. Medburn Street once continued west across the school site, before turning sharply south as Barclay Street,

named after the brewing company Barclay Perkins (later amalgamated with Courage) and now buried beneath the extensive modern additions to the school. This evolved out of the Victorian Medburn Street Board Schools (p 64), and was known from 1958 as Sir William Collins School, after the first chairman (in 1904) of the LCC's Education Committee. In 1991 it became Camden's first 'community school', where children and parents, from a multicultural and substantially Bangladeshi community, were to learn alongside each other.

The east side of Charrington Street comprises, at what are now **Nos.1–65**, three pleasingly complete terraces, dating from 1842–50. The houses are now divided into flats, so that each door in the street now bears two numbers. **Nos.42–65**, to the north of Medburn Street, are Listed, as are their railings. An early resident at No.74 (now **Nos.57–58**) was George Samuel Meason, a wood engraver and compiler-publisher of railway guides. Turn left (and south), however, noting that many of the first-floor windows are dignified by pediments. Most of the houses here have lost their original iron balconies, and plain modern replacements are the order of the day.

First developed as an extension of Ossulston Street, Charrington Street has been separated from the latter by modern traffic-calming measures. Where the road becomes a footway, we re-enter Somers Town proper, crossing the original

11 Edith Neville addressing an open-air meeting in 1939

alignment of Aldenham Street (p 59). This once ran across the whole width of the Town from Eversholt Street to Pancras Road, but has been progressively shortened. To your right it has been demoted to a footpath; and its easternmost end was sacrificed to the Purchese Street coal depot; while the intervening section, on your left, lies beneath the modern, single-storey buildings of the **Edith Neville Primary School**. Named after the ubiquitous local reformer (Fig 11), who died in 1951, this is the successor to the Aldenham Street Board Schools, opened on the north side of the site in 1874 and remodelled in 1909. Like many inner-city schools, where space was at a premium, it had a playground on the roof.

The construction of the new school (c.1972) saw the loss of the Shepherd & Shepherdess pub, which stood on your left. Also at this now extinct end of Aldenham Street, on the south side at No.49, was the 19th-century Aldenham Hall, for many years before WW II the gospel hall of the Christian Men's Union. No.16, nearby, had been the meeting-place in 1848 of the Camden Town branch of the Mormon Church.

Continue across the pedestrian area, passing on your right one side of Polygon Road Gardens (p 55). Beyond the open space, we reach **POLYGON ROAD**, known as Hampden Street until 1937. In the earliest days of Somers Town, before its rapid decline, there were actually detached villas here. The street housed not only refugees from the French Revolution but also some people who supported it. The London Corresponding Society, inspired by Thomas Paine, with 10,000 members, agitated for parliamentary reform and for the abolition of both the nobility and the clergy. Many of its members chose to live locally, close to town yet well away from the eagle eye of the authorities in Central London. Among them was John Gale Jones

(d.1838), who kept an apothecary's shop in nearby Wilsted Street. Tried for advocating republicanism, he was defended by Sir Samuel Romilly and acquitted. A radical 'Hampden Club' was established in Hampden Street soon after the Napoleonic Wars; later, in the 1830s, the area was regarded as a hotbed of Chartism.

To your left, on the south side of Polygon Road, is the red-brick **Hampden Nursery Centre**, run by Camden's Early Years Service. It stands on the site of what was, until after WW II, the Hampden Residential Club. Founded in 1882 to meet what the Duke of Westminster described as "a great want", and run by a company called Hampden House Ltd, it offered affordable accommodation for young trainee professionals, especially those 'up from the country'. The president was Viscount Hampden, whose portrait shared the Club's letterhead with that of John Hampden (1594–1643), the leading Parliamentarian mortally wounded in the Civil War. Other patrons included Lord Derby, Lord Shaftesbury, the MP and newsagent W H Smith, and Samuel Morley MP. The Club included a Masonic Temple and ran a dozen clubs and societies, athletic, social and professional, with such appropriate names as the Circle of Science and the Chapter of Literature. Pageboys with brightly buttoned uniforms were recruited from local school leavers. The attractions of Somers Town for such

an institution were presumably the cheapness of the land, and its nearness to three mainline stations. Strangely, in an appeal for share capital in 1892, the Club saw fit to claim that "the effect of the Midland clearances…has been to make this neighbourhood one of the healthiest parts of London"(!).

More or less on the site of the Nursery Centre was a junction with the north end of long-vanished Middlesex Street. There stood the Presbyterians' Middlesex Mission, and its associated (British Society) day school, founded in 1849, in rooms above a stable, by Dr James Hamilton of the Regent Square church. In its "plain and neat" building were two ground-floor classrooms with a large hall above; the windows, even then, were protected against vandalism by wire guards. A leading light of the mission was the Rev. Zephaniah Banks Woffendale. Mancunian by birth, and educated by Quakers in Kendal, he had come to London at the age of 14 to work in the Railway Clearing House (p 60). He later took to street-corner preaching in Somers Town, and was eventually ordained. The mission hall and school were demolished in 1879, and activities were temporarily transferred to the Zion Chapel at Goldington Crescent (p 66). A new Somers Town Presbyterian Church was built, facing onto the north side of what is now Brill Place (to your left). Opened in 1882, with Woffendale as minister, it flourished there for over 70 years.

Continue southward along **OSSULSTON STREET**, on whose east side the Hampden Club erected six small blocks to accommodate its young men. Agincourt, Baltimore, Cleveland, Doncaster, Edinburgh and Frankfort Houses (a motley assortment of names) were alphabetically arranged along the street from south to north. By 1955 the Club had become a hostel for British Railways staff. In 1972 it was used to house Ugandan Asian refugees. Camden Council then acquired the site for a mixed development, including the Hampden (now Somers Town) **Community Centre**; and the flats of **Monica Shaw Court**, which shares entrances with the earlier Phoenix Court. Dr Shaw was a much loved GP who from her Eversholt Street surgery served Somers Town people for half a century, often waiving her fees in pre-NHS days.

The opposite side of Ossulston Street is lined by one side of **Walker House**. Part of the LCC's Ossulston Estate, it was named after Mr H de R Walker, a former councillor for St Pancras South East and chairman of the LCC Housing Committee. The block was built in two stages around a large courtyard on the site of Equity Buildings, a particularly mean street of single-storey dwellings. Notice how the later northern end (1936–7) is relatively routine and built in plain stock brick, while the earlier southern end (1929–30) is rendered, and more in the spirit of nearby Levita House (p 41). No.149 Ossulston Street, on the Walker House site, was once the Marquess of Hastings public house; Thomas Cubitt, the publican in 1863, cannot have been the well-known builder of that name, who had died in the previous decade. No.127, in the same terrace, served in 1911 as the offices of the anarchist *Freedom* newspaper.

At Phoenix Road, turn right to reach the southwest corner of Walker House and the rebuilt **Cock** pub, which the LCC relocated from the opposite (southeast) side of the junction with Chalton Street, when it built Chamberlain House. The stretch of Chalton Street to the north was at first known as Upper Evesham Buildings. It was soon renamed as the east side of Clarendon Square, in whose centre stood The Polygon, the highpoint of Leroux's early Somers Town development. ('Clarendon' was one of several aristocratic names arbitrarily assigned to local streets in the hope of attracting residents of the right class.) Continue west along Phoenix Road, which here formed the south side of Clarendon Square, then turn right along the west side of the square which since 1938 has been part of **WERRINGTON STREET** (p 57).

Pause here to contemplate the history of the site. The once famous building **The Polygon** (Fig 12) was begun in 1791–2 by Jacob Leroux, in partnership with a Tottenham Court Road carpenter called Job Hoare. Building work proceeded fitfully and was suspended in 1794. Hoare went bankrupt, and work on the unfinished building resumed only in 1799, the year of Leroux's death. Described as an "experimental building", the Polygon had 16 sides, around which 32 houses were arranged in pairs. Among their early occupants were many of the French émigrés who settled locally; a hundred of them were living here in 1810, earning the block the nickname of 'Brittany Bay'. The Abbé Carron (p 36) moved into No.1 (in the southeast corner) in 1799. The early Polygon and its surrounding square were also home to professionals, to skilled craftsmen such as piano makers, and to artists, including the figure engraver Edward Scriven and the Dutch portrait painter Samuel De Wilde.

No.29 The Polygon, on the east side, was home for a decade to the novelist and atheist philosopher William Godwin, at that time running a 'juvenile bookshop' in Hanway Street (Fitzrovia). In his *Political Justice* he condemned the institution of marriage as "the worst of all laws", but that did not stop him marrying twice. He moved across the road to The Polygon (from Evesham Buildings, p 38) on his marriage in 1797 to Mary Wollstonecraft (p 102), the proto-feminist and author of *A Vindication of the Rights of Woman*. Mary died in the

52   12 Clarendon Square, with the Polygon (left) and St Aloysius Church (drawing, 1850)

same year, shortly after giving birth to a daughter, Mary, the future wife of Shelley and creator of *Frankenstein*. Godwin remarried in 1801, to his neighbour at No.27, the enigmatic Mrs Mary Jane Clairmont, who moved in with her two existing offspring; 3-year-old Jane would later become, as 'Claire' Clairmont, the mother of Lord Byron's ill-fated natural daughter, Allegra. William Godwin Jr (b. 1803) and Fanny Imlay, Wollstonecraft's daughter from an earlier liaison, completed a most peculiar family in which none of the five children had the same two parents. All moved on in 1807 to Skinner Street, Holborn.

The Dickens family, on their eviction from Johnson Street (p 56) in 1827, took lodgings in The Polygon. Here, in *Bleak House*, Charles set the dilapidated "downtown" residence of Mr Skimpole, mentioning in passing "the poor Spanish refugees walking about in cloaks, smoking little paper cigars" (cf. p 37).

In 1891 The Polygon was demolished, to be replaced by Polygon Buildings, four austere, barrack-like blocks, aligned north–south across the site. Built by the Midland Railway Company, they were some recompense for the great loss of housing caused when the railway invaded the area, although many of those housed in the Buildings were railway employees. The porters who looked after the blocks wore Midland livery. The Buildings were in turn pulled down and replaced (1972–6) by red-brick, low-slung **Oakshott Court**, named after William (Bill) Oakshott, the Mayor of Camden who died in 1975. Stepped up in an L shape on two sides of a grassy open space, the flats were so designed (by P Tabori) that each one has a south-facing aspect.

The west side of the old Clarendon Square is now occupied by **St Augustine's House** (1939), part of the red-brick and white-faced Eversholt Estate of the SPHA. Like their other local blocks, the flats here supplanted run-down houses already taken over by the Society. The slums of Clarendon Court (or Place) were swept away in the Eversholt development, which was interrupted by the outbreak of WW II and finally completed only 30 years later.

Return to Phoenix Road and continue west past **St Joan's House**, noting the foundation stone laid in 1946 by the Bishop of London. Reaching **EVERSHOLT STREET**, turn right. **St Richard's House** was built in three stages between 1954 and 1967. A proposal by Ian Hamilton, the SPHA architect, to build a 16-storey block of flats here, had fallen foul of LCC planning policy and been abandoned. High site costs on the Eversholt Street frontage, previously lined by small shops, meant that development here would need to include a commercial element. The corner site (now occupied by Avis car rentals) was long a Blue Star petrol station, with an underground garage started before WW II and used as a bomb shelter during it. A little to the north, and above the doorway of **No.102**, is an attractive panel of 1963, carved by the sculptor Alan Collins and representing the life of St Richard, the 13th-century Bishop of Chichester. Recently merged with the Humanist Housing Association, the SPHA has its present headquarters in St Richard's House, which is on the site of No.96 Seymour Street, its pre-WW II address.

Beyond is **Hill-Wood House**, opened in 1970 by Wilfred Hill-Wood, then vice-president of the SPHA. Bridging **POLYGON ROAD**, into which we turn, the block includes the **Hillwood Centre**, a day centre for the elderly, opened in 1971 by *Steptoe & Son* actor Wilfred Brambell and now run by Age Concern Camden. **St Martin's House**, the small SPHA block on your right, was opened without ceremony in 1940 on the site of the very first houses ever purchased by the St Pancras House Improvement Society. The adjacent pub, the Jubilee, closed in 2001 but is being renovated. Although its sign had depicted Queen Victoria boarding a train, there had been a pub of this name here since at least 1826–7, so that the jubilee alluded to could not have been hers. On the corner opposite is another small SPHA block, **St Margaret's House** (1950). This end of Polygon Road was originally named Gee Street, presumably after local carpenter-builder William Gee. In early Victorian times, No.10 Gee Street housed the Training Seminary for Boarders & Day Pupils – "for the youth of both sexes, upon the plan of the Glasgow Normal Seminary" – where the curriculum included mental arithmetic "by the method of Pestalozzi". An advertisement for the school showed happy children swinging around a maypole.

Regaining former Clarendon Square, bear right and cross the road to inspect on the wall of Oakshott Court a brown plaque to Mary Wollstonecraft, erected by Camden Council in 1979 after pressure from Claire Tomalin, her biographer. The plaque was presumably placed where it would be most noticeable. As previously mentioned (p 51), Mr & Mrs Godwin's house was actually on the opposite side of the Polygon.

Turn left, cross over Polygon Road, and walk ahead for a few yards by the playground of **St Mary & St Pancras CE Primary School**. Facing us and dominating the playground, and covering the whole of the school's west wall, is the magnificent *Somers Town Mural*, an imaginative assemblage of images depicting three centuries of local history. A haymaking scene evokes the area's peaceful rural past; brick kilns, smoky factories and a railway viaduct intrude. All human life is here. The poet Shelley courts Mary Godwin on a little bridge across the River Fleet, spied on by Frankenstein's monster! Ragged children rub shoulders with their modern counterparts; chimney sweeps and washerwomen together with local personalities from Godwin, Wollstonecraft and Dickens through Elizabeth Garrett Anderson to the 20th-century activists of the SPHA.

Return to the corner and turn left along Polygon Road, where there is a helpful key to the mural's content on a poster on the school wall. First conceived by the Somers Town Environment Association, and commissioned by the GLC, the mural is the work of Karen Gregory, who first painted it over three summers (1984–6) on the school's *east* wall. It was threatened with destruction when the vacant plot it overlooked was needed for development. Claire Tomalin led a successful campaign to save the mural, which by 1995 had been repainted on the west wall by the original artist, with funding from the Gulbenkian Foundation.

St Mary & St Pancras Primary School was formed by a merger in 1951 of the two local church schools. St Mary's has its origins in the Polygon Infant School, an early Victorian offshoot of the Somers Town Chapel. To make way for its single-storey building a slice was removed from the north side of the Polygon 'cake'. The present larger premises were designed by the church architect Sir Arthur Blomfield and opened in 1896. Behind the schoolyard, and on the site of former Grenville Mews, are the low infants' and nursery buildings dating from 1969.

Walk east past the main school building. **Mary Wollstonecraft House** (1992), whose construction led to the demise of the first mural, contains nine flats for people recovering from mental illness, funded by the health authority and designed for the SPHA by Gordon Fleming. The block covers the site of No.20 Clarendon Square, which from c.1852 was Lord Shaftesbury's London Female Dormitory, a refuge for "unfortunate females from the streets or prisons"; and of No.19, which was later one of the Magdalen Mission's several local bases (see p 59).

Turn left along a stretch of **CHALTON STREET**, known originally as Union Street. Here in 1813 the French émigré, Général Darican, was killed when he and his horse fell headlong into a hole 20 feet deep, which had appeared during one of the River Fleet's regular inundations of the area. At **Nos.103–117** are flats and houses of 1989–90, designed by Jim Monahan for the Covent Garden Housing Project. On the corner of Aldenham Street (p 59) beyond is **Phyllis Hodges House** (1993), named in honour of a tireless worker for the SPHA for some 40 years, and its Estates Manager in 1973–5. The flats replaced the Lord Somers public house, one of the first buildings to be erected in this northern part of Somers Town. Developers of middle-class estates often built a church to attract builders; here a pub was a higher priority.

Opposite is the west side of **Polygon Road Gardens**, a post-WW II open space, re-landscaped in 2001. The new boundary railings, with their 'human hand' motifs, were designed with the help of local children. Here, too, is the entrance to an adventure playground, begun in the 1970s by the Plot 10 Community Play Project, and which in its early years included a small city farm. The project is still active, providing after-school play facilities.

Next, to the north, is the former **Anchor**, one of two local establishments which functioned c.1930 as 'restaurant-pubs' (see also p 35). Most local watering-holes were then "horrid little places" which encouraged insobriety. Both Father Basil Jellicoe and Miss Edith Neville were supporters of the Restaurant Public Houses Association (RPHA), whose aims were to open public houses with *seating*, and serving inexpensive wholesome food – places where even a clergyman would feel comfortable. Whitbread's were persuaded to refurbish the Anchor as a restaurant-pub, and it opened as such in 1929. Jellicoe became the licensee and moved in. An oak-panelled bar, by Hamilton, served only beer (no spirits), and drunkenness was taboo. Above was a restaurant where lunch could be had for 1s.4d. (7p). In its short life,

the restaurant-pub was blessed by the Archbishop of Canterbury, and royally visited by Queen Mary and the Prince of Wales. It was handed back to Whitbread's in 1933, when the RPHA gave up running pubs to concentrate on the training of aspiring licensees. The Anchor has now been converted as housing, but still sports its old pub sign.

Next door is the hangar-like **Somers Town Community Sports Centre**, built (1996–7) in the grounds of the South Camden Community School, jointly funded by University College and Camden Council, and run by a charitable trust.

Ahead on the left are the flats of the SPHA's **Sidney Estate** (1931–8), named after demolished Sidney Street that previously bisected the site, and referred to at the time as the 'Garden Estate'. Six blocks in stock brick surround a generously large courtyard with trees and play areas. Designed by Ian Hamilton, the flats were the first to be all-electric, and although spartan by current standards, were a far cry from the insanitary and overcrowded houses they replaced, where whole families had lived in a single room and children had slept five to a bug-infested bed. As you walk around the estate, don't miss the colourful ceramic roundels above some of the 2nd-floor windows, designed by the sculptor Gilbert Bayes and mostly featuring scenes from fairy tales. Bayes also designed the charming finials of the washing-line

supports in the drying-yards. Though all of these were lost in the later 20th century through vandalism or theft, they are now being gradually replaced as funds allow (see also p 35).

First on the left is **St Anthony's Flats** (1938), the last block to be completed. In its court (not visible) the washing-line posts sported devils. The rather grand, iron-gated forecourt alongside the block leads to **St Francis' Flats** (of 1932). Note the small statue of the saint and his donkey, and a ring of concrete posts, still bereft of their Bayes finials, which here had a *Mother Goose* theme – "four and twenty tailors went to kill a snail".

BRIDGEWAY STREET (left) was Bridgewater Street until 1937. Here, on 23 January 1930, Lord Monk Bretton (Chairman of the LCC) detonated a small charge of dynamite in the chimney stack of No.23 to signal the start of building work on the Sidney Estate. **St George's Flats**, the first to be built, were opened later that year by Lady Cynthia Colville, lady-in-waiting to the Queen. Walk halfway along the street to view the recently refurbished block. The north side of Bridgeway Street is lined by routine Camden Council flats of 1960, numbered but not named.

Returning to Chalton Street, turn left, passing on your right the twin Doric porticoes of **Sussex House**. Ahead, on the left beyond Cranleigh Street, is **Stibbington House**, inscribed *1930* and

named after former Stibbington Street
(p 64). Although contemporary with nearby
social housing schemes of the Council and
SPHA, both blocks appear (from the rate
books) to have been privately built.

Turn left along **CRANLEIGH
STREET**, known earlier as Johnson Street.
Developer John Johnson was official
paviour to the Somers Town Paving Board
in the early years of the 19th century.
Leroux died in 1799, and his property was
sold off in lots 3 years later. Johnson bought
the leasehold of most of northern Somers
Town. He sublet to various (often local)
builders who in turn erected the 2- and
3-storey terraced houses eventually to be
demolished in the various 20th-century
slum clearance schemes.

The eastern part of Cranleigh Street
is still cobbled, as if in deference to Charles
Dickens, who in 1825–7 lived with his
parents at No.29 (later No.13) Johnson
Street (Fig 13). Having ceased work at the
Charing Cross blacking factory, he was
now a pupil at the Wellington House
Academy, to which he walked each day via
Drummond Street. After Lady Day 1827
the family was evicted for non-payment
of rent and rates. Their house was acquired
in 1921 by the Rev. J Brett Langstaff
and the Children's Library Movement.
Here they opened the David Copperfield
Library, both for the use of poor local
youngsters and as a memorial to the
novelist. The house was given to

13 The house in Johnson Street where Charles Dickens lived as a boy

St Pancras Borough Council which, however, declined to take on the library, and it closed after 10 years for lack of support. The building was demolished. On its site are **Cranleigh Houses,** occupied today by Camden Council flats, though seemingly first built as a private venture. An inscription *GB 1934* on the small central gable records the date of erection and the initials (presumably) of the builder or original owner. The block, unusually, gave its name to the street when the latter was renamed in 1937.

Pause by the Victorian, terracotta-faced, **Neptune** pub on the corner of **WERRINGTON STREET**, which, as an old street sign on the corner of Cranleigh Houses suggests, once ran further northward. Werrington is a Cambridgeshire property of the Dukes of Bedford, on whose Fig's Mead estate the original Werrington Street lay. In 1938 the name was extended along its southerly continuation, previously known as Clarendon Street. Severed from the latter when Mayford flats were built, the northern part then discarded the Werrington name, leaving it stranded on the Somers estate where it does not belong.

Turn left by the pub and walk along the present Werrington Street. The west side is lined by Camden Council's **Somers Town Estate**, six stock-brick blocks with balcony access, built progressively in 1928–31 by St Pancras Borough Council. **Johnson House**

and **Clarendon House** took the names of the streets they then faced. Set back from the road is **Gladwin House,** commemorating Grace Gladwin, who in her will of 1860 bequeathed "the residue of certain stocks for the poor of Somers Town". Out of sight behind Clarendon House is **Morland House**, its name recalling the painter George Morland (1763–1804), whose studio was in Camden High Street. The block stands on the line of former Little Clarendon Street, which once ran north–south through the middle of the site, and was a notoriously poverty-stricken street. It was home in the 19th century to a colony of clay tobacco-pipe makers (see *Camden History Review* 20). Locals knew the street as 'Little Hell'; policemen were said to venture there only in pairs. It was later renamed Wolcot Street, after John Wolcot, *alias* Peter Pindar (p 23) who died in St Pancras. **Wolcot House**, one of the first two blocks to be built, was opened in 1928 by the Princess Mary. Despite the royal ceremony, 'economy' was the watchword here: the utilitarianism of these council blocks contrasts starkly with Hamilton's more ambitious work on the neighbouring Sidney Estate, which is on your left.

St Christopher's Flats, on the corner of Bridgeway Street, were begun in January 1931, when General Sir Ian Hamilton (a namesake of the architect) lit a bonfire made of old wood from demolished houses,

and giant effigies of a rat, flea, bug and cockroach were ceremonially burned (Fig 14, p 58). Note the glazed parapet of the SPHA nursery school (founded at the Charrington Hall, p 65), which moved onto the roof of the newly completed block. Renamed **St Christopher's Nursery School**, it was opened by Princess Arthur of Connaught in January 1932.

St Nicholas' Flats, the next block on your left, was completed 2 years later and blessed by the Archbishop of Canterbury. Sidney Street had been pulled down and its houses pulled down to enable its construction. The nursery school spread onto the roof of St Nicholas', where a roof garden was installed, with 'Hans Andersen' reliefs by Lady Allen and a fountain by Gilbert Bayes. In its heyday the garden boasted a paddling-pool and sandpit, eventually abandoned for health and safety reasons. Decent clothing for the children to wear was provided by a Guild of Needlework, which was founded in 1930 by Amy Gedge, and flourished until 1957; hundreds of garments were made each year. A financial burden to the SPHA by 1970, the nursery school was handed over to the ILEA. Under Camden Council, its successor, budgetary cuts forced its closure in 1992. Rescued through a partnership of various local bodies, it was reopened on 12 May (St Pancras Day) in 1997, and is now run by the Somers Town Community Centre. 2001 saw the reinstatement of the

58   14 Sidney Estate, 1931: effigies of vermin prepared for ceremonial burning

lost finials in the drying-yard here, recreated to Bayes' original design – a series of identical painted sailing-ships arranged in a circle around an elaborately embellished centre post. Alfred J Stothard, who lived on this site in 1821, at No.13 Clarendon Street, was Medal Engraver in Ordinary to His Majesty; his work was exhibited at the Royal Academy.

Beyond Aldenham Street, on the west side of the St Mary's school site, stood the main hall of the Magdalen College Mission. Founded at Oxford in 1883, the mission first came to Somers Town in 1908 to help in the outreach work of St Mary's Church (below). Father Jellicoe, its leader, opened the hall in 1924 at what was then No.5 Clarendon Street (later No.83 Werrington Street). Here were run a nursery school, a soup kitchen, and various clubs, including one for boys which Jellicoe had founded earlier in 'Little Hell'. Holidays were organised for the nursery school children, while older boys were helped to emigrate to Australia. Jellicoe headed the mission from 1921 until 1927, when he resigned to work full time for the SPHA, and was succeeded by the Rev. Percy Maryon-Wilson, later Vicar of St Mary's. The mission building was later lent to the Church for use as a community centre, and during WW II hosted various SPHA activities displaced from the Basil Jellicoe Hall (p 38), which was in use as a bomb shelter. Taken over by the ILEA in 1967, the Magdalen club-house closed 2 years later.

At the junction with **ALDENHAM STREET** are four rare early bollards, painted black and white and inscribed "Sommers Town 1817". They were first erected by the Somers Town Paving Board, the body then responsible for paving and lighting the estate. 'Aldenham' is another street name which is out of place, having originated on the Brewers' estate to the east. It was later extended west along former Grenville Street, where you currently stand. The original Aldenham Street then gradually vanished, leaving its name behind in alien territory.

Turn briefly east, past a second drying-yard graced by a duplicate set of Bayes galleons. Beyond are **St Michael's Flats**, opened by the Duchess of Gloucester in 1938, where dolphins once adorned the washing-line posts. Return westward, past the crossroads, to where the council flats of **Aldenham House** (1928) face onto the junior department of **St Aloysius RC Primary School** (also p 38). Note the three statues, of Christ, the Virgin Mary and St Aloysius, and a plaque recording the (far from evident) rebuilding of the premises in 1927–9. Iron railings line the school's former rooftop playground.

On the corner of **EVERSHOLT STREET** is the parish church of **St Mary the Virgin**, in rather grim, plain stock brick, with a square tower topped and flanked by pinnacles. For a better view, cross to the opposite side of the main road and walk a few yards along Barnby Street. Designed, like the new St Pancras Church, by William and Henry Inwood, though in a very different style, it was mocked by Pugin, while Pevsner called it "thin and papery". A parish church from 1868, it originally opened in 1826 as a chapel-of-ease, known as the Somers Town Chapel. Dickens worshipped there as a boy. The chapel was at first hugely popular, thanks partly to its controversial attempts at converting local Catholics; services at which they publicly renounced their faith filled the pews to overflowing. An early incumbent was the Rev. T J Judkin, whose hymnal of 1834 consisted wholly of hymns no longer than four verses of four lines, "a number sufficient for any tune to be sustained without wearying the congregation". Originally nicknamed Mr Judkin's Chapel, the church was later dubbed "the Cabbies' Church" because of the aid it offered to cabmen using the old Euston Station.

Returning to Eversholt Street, turn left and north, observing the offices, opposite on the corner of Aldenham Street, of the travel firm Spanish Speaking Services, coincidentally located in a district which once sheltered many Spanish refugees (p 37). John Johnson's back-street houses have all been swept away, but some of those he built later in what is now Eversholt Street have survived. **No.140** served after WW II as the SPHA headquarters. **Nos.140–158** were refurbished by the SPHA as the first phase of **Irene Barclay House**, opened in 1977 by Princess Margaret. (Mrs Barclay, the first ever female Chartered Surveyor, was SPHA Estates Manager until her retirement in 1972 after nearly 50 years of service.) Victorian shop-fronts were removed and stuccoed residential ground floors reinstated. **Nos.170–180**, to the north, with their curly 'balconets', were also renovated. Between the two ranges is **Rowley's** bar, formerly the Seymour Arms, which had a theatre licence in 1855–7; this was once Upper Seymour Street.

On this side at **Nos.163–203** is a long brick building, once part of the Railway Clearing House. Begun in 1842 with just two clerks, the Railway Clearing House was formally established by Act of Parliament 8 years later to oversee all transactions between the then numerous private railway companies. It dealt with through-ticketing and with the harmonisation of safety practices; its resurrection might be welcome today! 2,500 clerks were eventually employed, enough to support a thriving dramatic society which performed at the Cabinet Theatre, King's Cross. The taller part of the building is an extension of 1901–2; the remainder, designed by James B Stansby, dated from 1874–5. Despite its size, the present building was only an annexe. The main premises of 1849, designed by Philip Hardwick in a similar neo-Georgian style, stood south of Barnby Street and were demolished to make way for the new Euston station. Later known as Eversholt House, the surviving buildings were refurbished as offices in the 1980s, serving in 1992 as a temporary home for Britain's first cartoon gallery, the Museum of Cartoons. Though unlabelled as such, the block is known today as 'Carriage Row' and houses the Society and College of Radiographers.

Recrossing the road, continue north to the second set of traffic lights, where two left turns will bring you to Mornington Crescent station, and the start of Route 4 (or your Tube home!). Alternatively, turn back and walk along Eversholt Street to Euston Station.

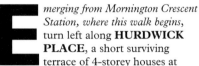

Route 4
Fig's Mead (Bedford New Town)

Emerging from Mornington Crescent Station, where this walk begins, turn left along **HURDWICK PLACE**, a short surviving terrace of 4-storey houses at the northern end of Hampstead Road. Hurdwick Farm lies near Tavistock on the Devonshire estate of the Russells, Dukes of Bedford. We are here at the north-western corner of what was once their Fig's Mead estate, a tract of farmland extending from the Hampstead Road east to what is now Pancras Road. Around 1826, with development of their better-known Bloomsbury estate almost complete, the Russells turned their attention to their more northerly property. They may have wished to create a second Bloomsbury here, but realising that 'first-rate' houses would not sell in such an outlying area, settled for what was meant to be a model middle-class suburb. Here, in 'Bedford New Town', there would be housing too for the better class of artisan or clerk. Crescents or squares would ensure that the area's character was superior to that of adjacent Somers and Camden Towns. Much thought was given to the names of the proposed streets, which it was decided would be borrowed from places on the Russells' estates in various parts of the country. The first plans for the new suburb, drawn up in 1826 by a Mr Stead, were radically revised in 1834 by Christopher Haedy, the Duke's London steward. His plans, in turn, needed further alteration when the London & Birmingham Railway cut a gash through the west side of the estate. Delayed first by this intrusion, and then by a building slump in the later 1840s, the development of Fig's Mead was not fully complete until 1859.

In its final form, the New Town consisted of three 'squares', none of which was even a rectangle! We soon reach **HARRINGTON SQUARE**. Its name honours Anna Maria Stanhope, daughter of the 3rd Earl of Harrington, who married the 7th Duke of Bedford in 1818. Lining the west side of the Square (though, strictly, in Hampstead Road) is **Greater London House**, until 1959 the Arcadia Works (or 'Black Cat' Factory) of the tobacco firm Carreras. Pevsner described the building, by M E & O H Collins (1926–9), as "abominable". In the recent (1998–9) restoration of the Egyptian-inspired façade, its two 10-ft-tall black bronze cats were reinstalled (in reproduction) at the main entrance, its fluted columns were re-exposed and repainted; and the series of whiskered feline faces beneath the roofline was reinstated.

15 Harrington Square photographed in September 1940, bus on end after bombing

Under the plans of both Stead and Haedy, Harrington Square would have been a crescent, balancing Mornington Crescent (on the Southampton estate), across whose garden enclosure the cigarette factory was controversially built. The Russells' new crescent was to be named Ridgmount Place, after Ridgmont (*sic*), a village adjoining Woburn Park, their Bedfordshire seat. By the time it materialised, the crescent had changed both its name and its shape. The triangular gardens were laid out in 1843.

Turn left along the Square's northeast side, a casualty of the German bomb which landed here in September 1940, opening a crater in the road and up-ending a double-decker bus (Fig 15). Eleven people lost their lives. The post-war St Pancras council flats of **Hurdwick House** fill the site of buildings damaged or destroyed. A terrace of original houses remains intact at **Nos.15–24**, with Doric-columned porticoes and, like most of the surviving houses on this walk, stuccoed at ground floor level. **Nos.17–18** have been knocked into one. No.18 was once the residence of Alexander M Bell (1819–1905), a Scottish-American educator and elocutionist who devised *Visible Speech*, a graphical representation of speech sounds based on the position of the vocal chords. Dr John Saunders Muir, vice-principal of the North London Collegiate School for Boys, lived at No.15 in 1855. E V Lucas, the

journalist, essayist and *Punch* contributor, lodged in Harrington Square in 1892. Here, too, was the first marital home of the physicist (Sir) Oliver Lodge (1851–1940), a pioneer of wireless telegraphy. The painter Walter Sickert moved to the Square on his second marriage in 1911.

Continue to the southeast corner, and the site, until 1893, of a Bloomsbury-style bar-gate, which protected the gentlefolk of the New Town from noisy horse-drawn commercial traffic. The gate was locked at night, and by day only gentlemen's carriages and cabs with fares were allowed to pass.

On the Square's south side (to your right), No.9 was home in the 1860s to Samuel Plimsoll, later (as an MP) famed for his promotion of the Plimsoll Mark or loading-line on ships, but then a local coal merchant (p 90). Despite public protests, No.9 and its neighbours were demolished by Camden Council in 1967–8. The roadway was moved southwards to align it with **LIDLINGTON PLACE** (on the left), providing a through route from Oakley Square (p 71) for southbound traffic emerging from the Camden Town one-way system. Likewise bereft of its houses, Lidlington Place is named after a village near another ducal property at Ampthill (Beds.). The marine painter Oswald Brierley lived at long-demolished No.8 in 1859.

South-westward lies Camden Council's

Ampthill Square Estate, a late-1960s development by Eric Lyons & Partners, combining low-rise, brick-built housing with three unmissable 20-storey tower blocks, distinguishable only by their late-1980s trimmings in different primary colours, and immortalised in paint of a different kind by local artist Frank Auerbach. All the blocks have Lake District names, Camden having continued the St Pancras Council policy of naming blocks in this part of the borough after Lakeland locations.

Cross carefully to the other side of the busy road and turn south along a footway to the left of red-trimmed **Oxenholme**, then fork right, and head straight towards the Telecom Tower on the skyline, with blue-topped **Gilfoot** to your right. At a children's playground, turn right, then left along a service road leading south. Walk slowly, for there is much history to absorb, and stop short of an eventual leftwards bend. Yellow-capped **Dalehead** (to your right) overlooks a stretch of Hampstead Road once known as Bedford Place, while a petrol station to the south beyond the railway cutting supplanted erstwhile Ridgmount Terrace. Twelve houses were erected hereabouts in 1838 by James Sim, the builder responsible for Bloomsbury's Woburn Square.

We are now approaching the site of another Bedford New Town 'square' which, despite fierce objection, was swept away in the 1960s. Its name, Ampthill Square, survives today only as a postal address. Stead's plan of 1826 would have placed here an elongated square with rounded ends, on an axis linking Euston Grove (p 24) with our starting-point. Haedy's 1834 revision proposed a 'Russell Crescent', aligned contrariwise SW–NE, and flanking a through route from Hampstead Road to Camden Street. With the advent of the London & Birmingham, plans were changed once again. When the crescent finally materialised, as Ampthill Square, in 1844–53, its gardens were bisected by the railway cutting, which its carriageways crossed over brick arches, replaced in 1896 by girders. Much of the Square's east side was lined by carriage sheds of the LNWR.

Further south, and also bridging the railway, was a short-lived Wriothesley Street, running east-west between Hampstead Road and what is now Eversholt Street. (Wriothesley was the family name of the 17th-century Earls of Southampton, whose Bloomsbury estate the Russells acquired by marriage.) The eponymous street was closed in 1846–7.

Ampthill Square was built on Pond Field, which had long been farmed, along with nearly 300 acres elsewhere in the parish, by the influential Rhodes family. William Rhodes, who came to London from Staffordshire in 1720, became an Overseer of the Poor. His grandson Thomas, a notorious St Pancras vestryman, was the great-uncle of Cecil Rhodes, who raised the family memorial in the parish churchyard. Rhodes' Farm lay just off Hampstead Road over to your right; the farmhouse somehow survived until c.1943.

The service road you are following is a 1960s extension of **BARNBY STREET,** which once linked Ampthill Square with Eversholt Street. To minimise contact between the New Town and Somers Town, there were only three access points on the former's eastern side, including this one, which offered Ampthill Square residents a route towards the City and the Inns of Court. Originally called Bedford Street, it was renamed in 1896 after Sir Joseph Barnby, the eminent organist and choral conductor and composer, best remembered for his part-song *Sweet and Low*; he died that year.

Ahead of you, the street bends leftward, to pass **Stockbeck** and **Beckfoot** flats, the latter on the site of a Russell Arms pub. Before the bend, however, turn left through a gap in the wooden palisade. As you approach **Brathay**, turn left (following the sign '1–4') then right. Soon, on your left, set in the turf at the foot of a flight of steps, is the only remaining physical reminder of Ampthill Square: a stone slab inscribed "Boundary of Ampthill Square Public Open Space". Officially open only to residents, the gardens were notoriously grimy, despoiled by the smoke from the railway bisecting them.

The Square was once inhabited by a number of minor authors and artists, and several notable thespians. At No.19, in 1859–64, lived Frederick Robson, a master of burlesque at the Olympic Theatre in Wych Street, Aldwych (see *Camden History Review* 8). Fellow actor (and child prodigy) William Henry West Betty, who lived at No.37 from 1857 until his death in 1874, was nicknamed the 'Young Roscius' after a sensational stage debut in 1802 at the age of 11. No.20 was the home (1904–13) of the Rev. Charles Silvester Horne, minister of the Whitefield Chapel in Tottenham Court Road, later an MP, and father of the BBC radio comedian Kenneth Horne (1907–1969). No.1 was home, from 1912, to the School for Mothers (p 41), which later became the St Pancras Maternity & Child Welfare Centre.

Continue east, between **Mickledore** and **Glenridding**, then turn left along an unnamed service road, lined on its opposite side by a 1980s rear extension to the former Railway Clearing House (p 60). **Calgarth** flats, on the left, cover roughly the site of Houghton Place, a short street which once joined Ampthill Square to the south-east corner of Harrington Square, and which took its name from Houghton House, a Bedford property at Ampthill. Living at No.2 Houghton Place in 1861–5, with her thespian mother, was Ellen (Nellie) Ternan, the young actress with whom Charles Dickens fell passionately in love as his marriage failed and to whom he left £1,000 in his will. The same house was occupied, in 1911-3, by the painter Spencer Gore. He and Sickert were thus near neighbours in 1911, the year when they, with others, established the Camden Town Group of artists. From the window or balcony of No.2 Gore painted several of his well-known works, including *Down the Garden* and *A London Sunset* (see *Camden History Review* 13).

Turn right, to emerge into **EVERSHOLT STREET**, this part of which was at first named Crawley Street, after Husborne Crawley, a village 2 miles from Woburn Abbey. Crawley Street was later absorbed into Seymour Street (the section to the south), which in turn merged in 1938 with its northern extension (beyond the traffic lights). The latter had always been known as Eversholt Street, after the nearest village to the ducal seat.

To your left, above shops, are **Holmrook** flats, of 1973. They cover the site of a baker's shop at No.219 Upper Seymour Street, long run by the Stanley family. With ovens extending beneath the pavement, this was reputedly, at the time of its closure in 1966, the last surviving underground bakery in the old borough of St Pancras.

Cross to the opposite side of the street, where once stood the Duke of Bedford public house. Whereas pubs were almost non-existent on the Bedfords' Bloomsbury estate, in the New Town there were several, each bearing a Russell-family title. Pass through a square-cut opening into the precincts of **Mayford,** a labyrinthine complex of low-rise, brown-brick maisonettes, completed in 1972, and covering the site of Crawley Mews. Beyond a tiny children's playground, turn right down a short flight of steps, then left along an unnamed, garage-lined service road. Visible almost opposite to your right is the Neptune pub at the end of Werrington Street (p 57), which once continued north-eastward from here until truncated when Mayford flats were built.

Continue along the service road, noticing the thick brick wall on your right. Behind a large tree is a stone plaque proclaiming that "This fourteen-inch wall is the property of the Duke of Bedford, 1861". The purposefully erected barrier was a potent symbol of the great social divide between the middle-class New Town and the Somers Town slums to the south.

We emerge into **CHALTON STREET** (also p 39) alongside the Victorian-tiled Eastnor Castle pub, whose name, that of Lord Somers' Herefordshire seat, confirms that we are indeed on the old Bedford–Somers boundary. Originally called Union Street, this northern part of Chalton Street began as a cul-de-sac. A turnstile at its dead end gave access to two official footpaths running diagonally across Fig's Mead to either end of what is now Crowndale Road; and to an unofficial path to Camden Street which locals used 'by sufferance' of the Duke of Bedford. Only those engaged in carpet beating were allowed to trespass on the ducal grass.

Union Street was later extended northwards and renamed Stibbington Street, after a Russell property in Huntingdonshire near the family's hall at Thornhaugh near Peterborough (cf. Thornhaugh Street, Bloomsbury). On the east side today are the surviving Victorian buildings of the Medburn Street Board Schools. They first opened around the corner in Werrington Street in 1873, apparently taking over the British School there. The next building, opened 4 years later, was approached from the east by Medburn Street (p 49), hence the schools' best-known name. The building here in Chalton Street dates from 1880, witness one of several plaques placed high up on the front wall. The inscription for the old "Boys" entrance also survives, while further plaques record another of the schools' successive titles. In 1904 they became the Stanley Schools, after Lyulph Stanley (Lord Stanley of Alderley), the last vice-chairman of the London School Board. With 2,000 pupils and an annexe in

Camden Street, the Medburn school became the largest in the borough. Before WW I the premises also housed the St Pancras School of Art. The 'Stanley' name was later dropped and transferred to the new Central Schools in Camden Street. The Board school evolved eventually into the present South Camden Community School. The Chalton Street building is now Camden Council's **Medburn Centre**, containing LEA offices, an LEA training suite, and the Somers Town Youth Club.

To the left, on the corner to the north of the old school, is the site of the Tavistock Arms, one of the two 'restaurant pubs' inspired by Basil Jellicoe (see also p 55). It was opened in that guise in April 1930 by Prince George (later Duke of Kent), who then walked up the street to the Anchor, accompanied by an enthusiastic crowd of locals. Less successful than its sister establishment, the Arms was soon forced to close when its manager Mr Sharpington fell ill and no replacement could be found.

Chalton Street now continues to the right as a footpath, along what was once the southern pavement of the *original* Werrington Street. Its roadway lies beneath the grounds of post-war Godwin Court. Walk along the footway to where the carriageway resumes. On the left here once stood the Bedford New Town Day Schools of the British Society; and the Bedford Independent (or Congregational)

Chapel, erected by the Congregational Building Society and opened in 1851. The poet Robert Browning was a regular worshipper there for several years. Though restored in 1885, it was closed in 1908 and rebuilt as the Charrington Hall, successively home to a Conservative Club and, in 1930, SPHA's newly founded nursery school. From that same year it was licensed as a 'little' theatre. The St Pancras People's Theatre had been founded 4 years earlier at the Mary Ward Settlement in Tavistock Place by the energetic Edith Neville, who served as its director. Removed to the Charrington Hall, its repertory company staged three performances each week, with a change of programme weekly. Compared to that of the nearby, and unrelated, Unity Theatre (below), its repertoire was fairly mainstream, including both light comedy and serious drama, from Shakespeare to Chekhov. The building was destroyed in an air raid in 1940.

Charrington Street (p 49) now intersects from the right. Until WW II this junction was a crossroads; Charrington Street continued north to a junction with Crowndale Road. On the corner opposite is a porticoed house, formerly No.80 Charrington Street, but now numbered both as Nos.63-65 Charrington Street and **Nos.144-148** Chalton Street. It once housed the St Pancras Committee of the Charity Organisation Society (now the

Family Welfare Association), and in 1924 hosted the inaugural meeting of the St Pancras House Improvement Society (later SPHA).

The road along which we continue eastward is still, officially, a detached part of Chalton Street. On the right we encounter **Unity Mews**, a modern development of 15 houses and flats, built by SPHA on the site of the old Zion Chapel (below). The Unity Theatre moved here in 1937, a year after its formation in Britannia Street, King's Cross. 400 volunteers collaborated in converting the old chapel for theatrical use. For some 40 years, the Unity was renowned for its quality amateur productions of left-wing drama. It served as a training-ground for numerous well-known theatrical figures, including Lionel Bart, Alfie Bass, Michael Gambon, Bob Hoskins, David Kossoff, Warren Mitchell and Ted Willis. The black American singer Paul Robeson, then an international superstar, appeared at the Unity in 1938, unpaid and as an ordinary member of the cast. Renovated in 1966-8, the theatre was gutted by fire in 1975 By 1983 most of the company had dispersed, but productions continued at various other venues, including the Lord Palmerston (p 17). A circular plaque, recalling this "theatre run for the people by the people" is mounted by the entrance to Unity Mews, declared open in 1992 by Bill Owen, another of the theatre's 'alumni'.

We soon reach **GOLDINGTON CRESCENT**, built on the eastern edge of a field called 'Little Fig's Mead', and taking its name from a village near Bedford. One 19th-century source asserts that this spot was traditionally known as Gooseberry Green, and had reputedly been "one of the worst resorts of bad characters". The reason for the name is unclear. Maybe stalls selling gooseberry fools were set up here to tempt patrons of the nearby Adam & Eve pleasure gardens (p 98), just as they were near the gardens' namesake at Tottenham Court (p 14), where the fabled Gooseberry Fair was held. Although the Crescent's first houses appeared only in 1849–50, its enclosure may have been laid out earlier, appearing on Britton's 1834 parish map as an elliptical patch of green. Four years before that, a builder called Soward had been seeking leave to develop 'The Oval', as he called it. In 1854 an address in the Crescent was a temporary home to the St Pancras National School for Girls while it awaited completion of its new building.

At the north end of the crescent is the **Prince Alfred**, a modern rebuild of a pre-war public house which had stood nearby on the south side of Crowndale Road, and was named after Queen Victoria's second son. Ahead is Goldington Crescent Gardens, overlooked by the tall buildings of St Pancras University Hospital (p 97). Turn right past **Nos.5–16**, the one range of

houses here to survive heavy wartime bombing. These have been knocked together as flats, so that between the 12 addresses there are only five doorways; the Camden Council project won a Civic Trust award in 1961. Norah Murray (d.1989), who lived at **No.11**, was nicknamed the 'Russian Queen of St Pancras': recruited as a Soviet spy, she had been the first Russian war-bride to come to England in 1942.

Beyond No.5, turn into **GOLDINGTON STREET**. Nearby, on the right, a locked metal gate guards an old alleyway, which once led to No.1 Goldington Street. Tucked away behind Goldington Crescent, this was built as Zion Chapel in 1852 by the Rev. James Nunn as a replacement for the old Baptist place of worship in Chapel Street (p 44). The new 'Zion Chapel' was later taken over by the Presbyterians, after the demolition of their Middlesex Mission hall, and served as their Goldington Crescent Church until their new 'Somers Town' building was ready. The minister, the Rev. W Ewart, was noted for the mission services he held in the railway arches on Pancras Road. From 1884 the Zion Chapel was occupied by the Aldenham Institute, founded in Aldenham Street (p 50) two years earlier by the Rev. Woffendale, for the "social, mental and religious improvement" of young men over 15. Besides Bible classes and prayer meetings,

it offered a wide range of sporting activities, and an educational programme covering subjects both academic and practical, from the '3 Rs' to violin-playing and plumbing. The institute closed in 1900, and the building was later acquired by the Unity Theatre.

The east side of Goldington Street is today dominated by one side of post-WW II Cecil Rhodes House. Underlying the block is a field once known as 'The Slip': bordering the flooding-prone River Fleet, it was doubtless often waterlogged. A square-cut opening offers a view through Cecil Rhodes House to the old parish church. It also marks the site of *pre-war* Chenies Place, which here ran east from Goldington Street to debouch into a stretch of Pancras Road once known as Chenies Terrace. (Chenies, near Amersham, was once a Buckinghamshire seat of the Dukes of Bedford.)

The original houses on the east side of Goldington Street were built on Bedford land, but seem to have soon been sold to the Brewers' Company, the owners of the opposite side of the street. Here there survives, at **Nos.26–39**, a pleasing terrace of early Victorian 3-storey houses, built in a style typical of the Brewers' estate. Back on the east side, and almost opposite Platt Street, there once stood the Star public house at No.10, which in 1866 functioned as a music hall (Fig 16). By 1870 the Goldington Street name had been extended south along former Brill Street as far as what is now Brill Place (p 44). Twenty years later, this southern section was largely covered by the Midland Railway's two-level coal depot, and replaced by a new Purchese Street (p 48) on a more westerly alignment.

Follow this for a few yards before pausing at the corner of **CHENIES PLACE.** Dating from 1949, this replaced the lost eastern end of Platt Street, and borrowed its name from the nearby pre-war Chenies Place. The new street cut through the site of bombed Metropolitan Buildings, London's first ever purpose-built flats, and the capital's first block of 'model dwellings' for the 'deserving poor'. (For more details, see *Camden History Review* 20.)

Financed under the system known as '5% philanthropy' they were built in 1847 by the Metropolitan Association for the Improvement of the Dwellings of the Industrious Classes, of which Dr Southwood Smith was a leading light. The architect was William Bonython Moffatt, once a partner of Sir George Gilbert Scott. The Buildings comprised 110 two- or three-roomed flats, built as a range of eight distinct double houses, facing north onto Platt Street, with two projecting wings (Fig 17, p 69). The flats were built to a high standard: accessed from an internal staircase, each had running water, a scullery and WC. The rents were too high

16   Star Music Hall poster, 15 February 1866

to attract the poorest people for whom the dwellings had originally been intended. Most early residents were respectable, better-off working people, and some were even middle-class. Robert Ablett, a porter's son, and the founder of the Royal Drawing Society, lived at No.108 Metropolitan Buildings in 1848–50.

From the 1850s, the site was known as Pancras Square. In April 1941, a parachute mine landed in Pancras Square, causing 200 casualties and 77 deaths. The devastated Buildings were demolished, and a new Chenies Place was opened up across the site. On its northwest corner is the modern **Doreen Bazell Hall**, its entrance topped by a miniature glass rotunda serving as a skylight. This is the tenants' hall for residents of two nearby blocks of council flats, whose Pancras Road frontages we shall shortly observe. Doreen Bazell (d.1994) was secretary of the tenants' association and a pillar of the local community.

Walk east along Chenies Place, and turn left along **PANCRAS ROAD** (see also p 88). Its west side here is overlooked by two cliff-like blocks of flats, named **The Chenies** and **Cecil Rhodes House**. Dating from 1948–50, both were designed for St Pancras Council by Thomas Sibthorpe; in both, the glass-fronted stairwells and lift-shafts serve as a pleasing vertical architectural feature. Cecil Rhodes House was briefly known as 'Grangefield',

after a local meadow, but the council changed its mind. The field name was transferred to a different block in Marquis Road, Camden Town, while the Pancras Road building was renamed in honour of the founder of Rhodesia (p 101). In 1983 Camden councillors took exception to the colonialist name, proposing to rename the block yet again, a move scotched by objections from residents. Suggested replacement names had been Zimbabwe Court and Robert Mugabe House. *Still* Cecil Rhodes House, the block was home in 1986 to the journalist John McCarthy, just before his fateful journey to Beirut and his 4-year incarceration there as a hostage.

Part of the site was once occupied by the large St Pancras Iron Works, which specialised in high-class fittings for stables and functioned here for some 40 years from 1864. In that same year, the landlord of the Crown, which stood just to the north on the corner of Goldington Crescent, applied unsuccessfully to the Vestry to install a horse trough outside his pub, to cater for the increase in traffic along Old St Pancras Road after the removal of the turnpike gates which had stood outside the churchyard opposite. Traffic certainly did increase: by the next decade there was a regular omnibus service between Kennington and Kentish Town which passed along the road. This was soon supplemented by horse-drawn

trams from Holborn. When the line was electrified in 1909, a new link was installed along Crowndale Road (see below), enabling the Pancras Road trams to traverse Camden High Street.

On regaining Goldington Crescent, cross the gardens to their north end, and there observe a horse trough which was erected, by the Metropolitan Cattle Trough & Drinking Fountain Association – a reminder of the days when countless horses were employed locally to serve the various goods and coal depots.

Look across to the north side of the Crescent and to red and yellow-brick **Goldington Court**, set around a courtyard, behind a monumental archway guarded by massive security gates. Built in 1904–5 as Goldington Buildings, this was the first block of flats to be erected by St Pancras Council. Councillor George Bernard Shaw is said to have been among those who campaigned for their construction. An early resident, at No.17B Goldington Buildings, was Ethel Le Neve, the secretary and mistress of the dentist Dr Crippen. A Camden-born girl, she lived there with her parents at the time of her ill-fated affair with the wife-poisoner – midway between their New Oxford Street workplace and the Crippens' home in Hilldrop Crescent (off Camden Road), where the poisoning took place in 1910. The block stands on the site of the Elephant & Castle pub in St Pancras Way (p 97) and a timber yard; the

17 Metropolitan Buildings, Pancras Square (drawing from *The Builder*, 1847)

River Fleet flowed between them. Acquired in 1825 by the builder Thomas Cubitt, the timber-yard site seems never to have been developed for housing, perhaps for fear of flooding.

Once bridging the river here, and leading off westward, was a thoroughfare forming the northern boundary of the Fig's Mead estate, known as Fig Lane and first made up in the 17th century. Here was found the empty coffin of thief-taker Jonathan Wild, after its exhumation from the nearby churchyard in 1725. Turn left along the south side of **CROWNDALE ROAD**, as Fig Lane has been known since 1863, after tolls were removed. (Crowndale Farm was another Russell property near Tavistock, and the reputed birthplace of Sir Francis Drake.)

The opposite side of the road at this eastern end was at first named College Terrace, after the nearby veterinary college, on the edge of whose paddock it lay. At the end of Royal College Street stood the College Arms, a large and elegant Victorian pub, whose post-WW II replacement, the **College Bar,** has all the charm of an oversized portacabin. At **Nos.2–22**, routine late-1960s council flats and shops cover the site of an erstwhile row of small shops. Nos.18–24, known collectively as Cantlowes House, and dating from c.1825, were attributed to Thomas Cubitt, the developer of College Place, which here once opened into Fig Lane, close to a turnpike gate. Although

Cantlowes House was among the earliest buildings to be Listed, its status did not save it from demolition. It took its name from the medieval manor of Cantelowes (or Cantlowes), which extended north from here to Highgate. In the 18th century the manor came into the possession of Charles Pratt (Earl Camden), on whose land was developed the earliest part (from 1791) of 'Camden Town', to the east of the High Street, and from Fig Lane northwards. Terraces on the later-built south side of the Lane took the names of Bedford properties – Wansford Place (after a village near Thornhaugh) and Maulden Place (after another near Ampthill). There today (on your left) are two large St Pancras Council blocks built on the site of houses badly damaged in WW II: **Crowndale Court** (1958), and the even more massive 6- to 8-storey **Godwin Court**, named after William Godwin (p 51), which in the 1960s housed Camden's local children's library.

Surviving opposite at **No.26** is red-brick "Old Church House 1897 AD" (see inscription), actually built as the *new* mission-house and vicarage for the nearby old parish church. The original building on the site, sometimes known as Crowndale Hall, had served variously as a theatre of the nearby vets' college, as a nursery, and as the parish's first, hopelessly cramped, coroner's court. No.26 now houses **Theatro Technis**, a theatre and cultural

centre for the Greek-Cypriot community. Founded in 1957 as the Greek Arts Theatre Club, it initially used various venues, including the redundant Freightliner depot in York Way, before settling down in Crowndale Road in 1978. "More than a theatre", it also runs a library and luncheon club. Surmounting the Mannerist style doorway is a small figure of St Pancras, the teenage Roman martyr. The original effigy, by the sculptor H Hems, was stolen in 2000, and for over a year its niche was occupied by a potted plant. A replica statuette, carved by Jim Staines, was unveiled in June 2001.

Beyond the next traffic lights, pause at the northeast end of Oakley Square. To your right, on the corner of Camden Street, is the still thriving **Working Men's College** (now 'for Men & Women'). Founded in 1854 by the Christian Socialist Frederick Denison Maurice, along with Charles Kingsley and Thomas Hughes, this first occupied a house in Holborn's Red Lion Square, before moving to Great Ormond Street. The many eminent early teachers at the college included artists John Ruskin, Ford Madox Brown and Dante Gabriel Rossetti, while later lecturers included Darwin and T H Huxley. In 1904, the Prince of Wales laid the foundation stone for this more spacious building in Crowndale Road, into which the college moved a year later. Designed by W D Caröe in (for him) an uncharacteristically sober neo-Georgian style, built in deep-red brick and surmounted by a white louvred 'lantern', it boasted 30 classrooms, laboratories and a gymnasium. An extra floor was added in the 1930s.

Continue to the next zebra crossing, passing (on your right) a terrace built by 1801 on the southern edge of Lord Camden's estate, and long known as Gloucester Place. A companion terrace to the west, past Bayham Street, was pulled down in 1900 to make way for the theatre on the corner beyond, serving today as the Camden Palace nightclub. On the intervening corner is the **Hope & Anchor** pub, which after a period as 'Clutterbucks', has reassumed its original, 18th-century name. Overlooking Crowndale Road is a life-sized figure of a sailor with an anchor over his shoulder and holding in his hand a globe-shaped lamp.

The terraced houses on your left at **Nos.31–53** were built in the 1840s as part of the Fig's Mead development. Listed Grade II, they have recessed sashes and delicate cast-iron balconies.

Return now to **OAKLEY SQUARE**, Bedford New Town's third and last inaccurately named 'square', this time a somewhat angular crescent. Under Haedy's 1834 plan (p 61) there would have been no open space here. Streets of terraced houses would have criss-crossed Fig's Mead in an 'X' formation; and

18   Oakley Square, bar gates & lodge, with St Matthew's on the right (photograph, 1893)

71

the modern street map would have featured such unfamiliar names as 'Kingston Street' and 'Kingston Place'. From the later revision of Haedy's plans emerged Oakley Square, named after yet another ducal property in Bedfordshire, and developed gradually, in 1845–59. The Square's south side was demolished c.1965 to make way for new local authority housing, despite a vigorous public campaign to save it. Its roadway now carries fast-moving one-way traffic.

Until 1893 vehicular access to both sides of the Square was limited by two bar-gates here at its northeast end. One gatekeeper was responsible for all three local barriers. His single-storey lodge survives (Fig 18), stuccoed and Listed Grade II. Just visible through foliage above its Crowndale Road frontage is the Bedford coat of arms. Long used as a glorified garden shed, it was recently refurbished and, as **The Lodge**, is now occupied by a systems support company.

Turn right along the Square's quieter northwest side. The modern 5-storey block of flats named **St Matthew's Court** stands on the site of St Matthew's Church, part of whose ragstone churchyard boundary wall may still be seen rounding the corner into Crowndale Road. Designed in a Decorated Gothic style by John Johnson of the Adelphi (better known for his work at Alexandra Palace), the church was erected in 1852–6 on a site presented

by the Duke of Bedford. He gave £1,000 to the building fund, a quarter of it conditional upon the erection of a steeple. The spire, which was duly built, lost its pointed tip during WW II, when the church was severely damaged. Although restored, it was later declared redundant, and pulled down in 1977. Next door, at **No.52**, is a neo-Gothic building, now a private house, with a squat pyramidal steeple inexplicably topped by a gilded sailing-ship and a tiny golden yacht. A lamb-and-flag insignia above the doorway suggests a former religious use, and this was, indeed, the vicarage (1871) of St Matthew's Church, also by Johnson.

Nos. 53–69, beyond, form an apparently continuous range of partly stuccoed 'second-rate' houses, with Doric-columned porticoes. Above the first-floor windows, triangular and segmental pediments alternate, all flanked by small scallops (a Russell family emblem). Indicative of the Square's piecemeal construction is **No.57**, a curious, narrow-built intruder of only 3 storeys and in a homelier style. George Rowney, the manufacturer of artists' materials, was living here in 1861.

As you walk along, note the series of coal-hole covers set in the pavement, some bearing the names of several local ironmongers — T Sampson of Euston Road, Moore of Somers Town,

Jennings of Great College Street, and Beach of Camden Town.

Glance left across the Square's pleasantly leafy **gardens**, first laid out in 1845 and ceremonially reopened, after wartime damage, in 1953. Beyond them, on the long-demolished south side of the Square, the philosopher Herbert Spencer lived at No.24 in 1859; and Lenin occupied a flat at No.6 in 1911 while on a visit to London. No.1 (at the southwest end) was, from 1908, the headquarters of Magdalen College Mission (p 59), serving later as the first registered office of the St Pancras House Improvement Society. At the far end of the Square turn right, noting that the section of Eversholt Street into which we emerge is actually labelled "Oakley Square" and that porticoed **Nos.71–76** opposite are numbered as part of the latter. **No.72**, in the 1960s, was the headquarters of International Voluntary Service.

North of these, **EVERSHOLT STREET** resumes, its west side lined, at **Nos.235–277**, by a plain terrace of old 4-storey houses, with small shops and eating-places on the ground floor, and a continuous range of curly iron balconies above. Opposite, on this side of the street, at **Nos.210–214**, are the premises of funeral directors Leverton & Sons (see *Camden History Review* 10). Founded in 1789 in Henry Street (on the Regent's Place site, Euston Road), the prestigious family firm moved to Eversholt Street in 1888. When, in 1933, they acquired their first Rolls-Royce hearse, its earliest passengers included none other than Henry Royce, whose body was brought from Sussex to London for cremation. More recently the company organised the funerals both of Diana, Princess of Wales (1997) and of Queen Elizabeth, the Queen Mother (2002).

Previously based a little to the north, Leverton's were forced to move to their present site when what is now the **Crowndale Centre** was built in 1912. This massive block, in red brick and stone, now houses various departments of Camden Council; while **Camden Town Library** occupies part of the ground floor, having moved here from the High Street in 1996. The main building was converted in 1987–8, to the award-winning plans of Charles Thomson of Rock Townsend. It had previously served as the (second) North West District postal sorting office, whose predecessor had stood a few doors to the south. Running once beneath Eversholt Street, and linking the sorting office with Euston Station, was the first phase of the Pneumatic Dispatch Railway. Constructed in 1863–5, and using compressed air, it carried mailbags in trucks through horseshoe-shaped tunnels just $4^1/_2$ ft high. A further section was opened later, running via Holborn to the City. Built as a speculative private venture,

the railway was not a success: its tunnels leaked, and having failed to impress the Post Office, it was abandoned in 1874.

A large metal gate marks the entrance to former Eversholt Mews, now occupied by the Crowndale Centre's car-park and its modern health centre annexe. Beyond, on the corner with Crowndale Road, and still adorned by a fearsome lion's head, is the former Camden Town Post Office, relocated to the High Street in the 1990s. Camden Council's Housing Department has now moved in.

Cross Eversholt Street here at the traffic lights. Facing the well-known Richard Cobden statue (see *Camden History Review* 9) is diminutive **MILLBROOK PLACE**, its name a final reminder that we are still in Bedford New Town: Millbrook is another village near Ampthill. No.1 was home to the alliteratively named Claude Clarke Claremont, the public vaccinator for St Pancras, who died in 1900. Only one of the original houses survive, the others were pulled down for the building of **Mornington Crescent Station**, opened on the 'Hampstead Tube' in 1907. After a lengthy closure for refurbishment, it reopened in 1998, its oxblood-red tiles restored, and its interior tiling reproduced from Leslie Green's original designs. The reopening ceremony was performed by cast members of BBC Radio 4's *I'm Sorry, I Haven't a Clue*. They returned on

17 March 2002 , unveiling a Comic Heritage plaque to the satirist Willie Rushton (1937–1996), a past master of the programme's spoof parlour game, 'Mornington Crescent', which has brought national 'fame' to this otherwise unsung part of North London.

King's Cross and the Railway Lands

This walk cannot be described as picturesque but is nevertheless full of historical interest, especially for those interested in industrial archaeology. Much of the area is under threat from the conversion of St Pancras Station to accommodate the new Channel Tunnel Rail Link (CTRL) terminal, and the work on its approach routes. As these works progress, you may find that sections of the walk are affected. The walk describes certain buildings extant at the time of writing (early 2002), but which may now be gone.

Leave King's Cross Underground station by the stairs marked "Thameslink and Kings Cross stations". Turn immediately left past a news stand, and walk towards St Pancras station, whose clock tower soars ahead. Note on the gable alongside it a black statue of Britannia. Stop before the pavement ends and turn to look at the front of King's Cross station behind the low, modern entrance buildings.

The King's Cross name derives from a memorial designed by Stephen Geary, architect of Highgate Cemetery, and erected on the site of the turnpike at the junction of three roads: the New Road

from Paddington to the City (now Euston Road); ancient Maiden Lane (now York Way); and the old road north from Gray's Inn (now Gray's Inn Road, which at that time swung left over Battle Bridge and then continued northwards into present-day Pancras Road). A memorial statue to the late King George IV perched high above a Greek Doric base, this 60-ft structure was completed in 1836 but soon removed, as a nuisance to traffic, in 1845. Yet it gave its name to an area that had for centuries been known as Battle Bridge, a crossing of the River Fleet. Traditionally, "Battle Bridge" recalled a wholly imaginary battle between Queen Boudicca and the Romans in 61 AD; more likely, the name was a corruption of Bradford or Broad Ford.

By the early 19th century the area was conspicuous for its dust heaps produced by, and brickfields needed for, the rapid urbanisation of this part of London. The scene is now dominated by **King's Cross Station**, erected by the Great Northern Railway (GNR). The GNR was incorporated by Act of Parliament in June 1846, its main purpose being to connect York with London. Because of a delay in acquiring the land, a temporary terminus was opened on 7 August 1850 on the west side of Maiden Lane (now York Way), whose site we shall visit later.

The plain brick exterior of the station was built in 1851–2 by Lewis Cubitt (1799–1883), brother of the more famous

builder Thomas. It is the oldest surviving railway terminus building in London. Its two semicircular lunettes, reflecting the arches of the train shed roofs behind, are separated by a 120-ft high clock tower topped by an Italianate roof. The clock, now chiming once more, is by Dent and was exhibited at the Great Exhibition of 1851. In that year *The Builder* recorded Cubitt's remark that "the building will depend for its effect on the largeness of some of the features, its fitness for its purpose and its characteristic expression of that purpose". Early photographs show the arcade that formed the lower part of the façade, but this became masked by a clutter of small buildings, huts and shelters, removed in the 1970s when the present covered concourse was built in front.

To your left, ahead, is the former Great Northern Hotel, added by Lewis Cubitt in 1854 and built on a curved plan to follow the original line of Pancras Road, which was later diverted to the west. The exterior has been refurbished, but the hotel closed in February 2001. It owed its longevity to its simple, hence easily maintained, layout and construction. Cubitt designed the hotel to look inwards (and away from the rather ramshackle terraced houses opposite, demolished in 1871) towards the station across a large garden, which has since been engulfed by extensions to the station. Built in a simple Italianate style, rather like a tall London terrace, it had 100 bedrooms. The *Official Illustrated Guide* to the GNR in the 1860s boasted that "good wines, excellent viands, lofty well ventilated bedrooms and extremely moderate charges are among the advantages of this first-class hotel". The cost of full board at 14s. [£0.70] a night was, however, in the upper range of contemporary London hotel prices.

In 1863 the world's first underground railway was opened from Paddington to Farringdon and a few months later, tunnel connections to it from the Great Northern were opened. Northbound underground trains had to negotiate the Hotel Curve, a notoriously dark, smoke-filled, greasy climb upwards (where on at least one occasion a train slid backwards into the one behind)

before having to reverse into the main station. Large-scale OS maps show the line's route as running neatly between the station and the hotel, and not under the hotel itself, as is commonly supposed.

Previously on the hotel's site were the Small Pox and Inoculation Hospitals, founded in July 1746 in Windmill Street (Fitzrovia), for the reception of infected

19 Small Pox Hospital (left; drawing, 1807). From the site of St Pancras Station, with a view of houses along the east side of present-day Pancras Road. The London Fever Hospital is to the right

patients with 'casual small pox' and for inoculation. They were housed in various buildings for several decades thereafter, including leased premises in Cold Bath Fields. In 1763 the freehold of 4 acres known as Drakefield at Battle Bridge was bought from a Mr Thomas Saltonstall, but as soon as the foundations of a hospital were laid, the local inhabitants of St Pancras, Kentish Town, Hampstead and Highgate took legal action. The Court ruled that if they could suggest another equally remote site, the hospital should move, but none was suggested. A new building opened just for inoculation on 9 December 1767. A separate Small Pox hospital was built alongside in 1793–4, after considerable repairs to the Cold Bath Fields Hospital were found to be needed and the lease there was relinquished. The first patients were admitted in June 1794. Vaccination was introduced there in 1799 by Dr William Woodville, a physician with the hospital for 14 years until his death there in 1805. Woodville had assisted Edward Jenner, the pioneer of vaccination, in his researches and was also the author of an influential book *Medical Botany* (1790).

In 1801 the London Fever Hospital was established and opened to patients in a separate building (to the west of the smallpox hospital, and along Pancras Road, Fig 19). Dr Southwood Smith served as a physician there in 1824. The hospital's "superior building materials" (e.g. a

Portland stone cornice and York paving) were auctioned off in 1850 after the GNR had bought the site of both institutions, offering £20,000 in compensation, and the removal of the Smallpox Hospital to Highgate Hill (on the site of the present Whittington Hospital). The London Fever Hospital moved to a new building in Liverpool Road, Islington in 1848, and later to Hampstead.

Walk past the side of the hotel along **PANCRAS ROAD** (p 88). Before the CTRL works started, Pancras Road used to continue straight ahead along the side of St Pancras Station. Beyond the Hotel it has now been diverted to the right, towards King's Cross Station (Platforms 9–11).

Pause where the road bends right. Before the coming of the railway this part of the original Pancras Road was known as Pancras Place. Here stood Paradise Row, erroneously described by several historians as being part of Agar Town (which lay further north). Houses built in this vicinity in the late 18th century had quickly deteriorated, and had by the Victorian period become an "awful rookery". A report of 1850 speaks of 16 houses in Pancras Place in a filthy state, never painted or repaired, each let to five or more families, with partially uncovered cesspools, and claims that if one of them was taken down all would fall. Fall they did within a few months, as this whole area was cleared by the GNR, who built stabling blocks on the site.

A description in 1851 of the area between the New Road (Euston Road) and the land as far north as the Regent's Canal (which we cross later) talked of "immense destruction" in preparation for the new terminus. All the little houses behind the hospital had been razed as well as properties on the west side of what is now York Way. The street layout behind the hospital was, however, largely retained in the rebuilding after King's Cross Station opened in 1852.

Now, at the start of the 21st century, immense destruction for another terminus (the extended Saint Pancras for the CTRL) is on the cards once more. During late 2001 the area between the Great Northern Hotel as far as Goods Way (beyond the gas-holder, ahead) was cleared and the atmospheric, cobbled streets so beloved of film makers were blocked off. Nearly all the mid-Victorian buildings which once lined the original Pancras Road past this point – which included industrial buildings and model dwellings – have been demolished.

Continue along Pancras Road to reach the corner of King's Cross Station. The new layout follows the line of the former Cheney Road (as Cheney Street was renamed in 1937) plus that of its predecessor, Pancras Walk, and of an even earlier Back Walk. As the road bends again, left, we reach a long brick wall. This is the exterior wall of King's Cross Suburban station, enlarged in the 1890s and again in

1924 to cater for expanding commuter traffic. It is difficult to picture now, but until very recently this section of former Cheney Road had a quintessentially Victorian feel, with its cobbled road surface, granite kerbs and cast-iron bollards. It was the setting for many films, e.g. *The Ladykillers* and *The Secret Garden*.

Before King's Cross was extended in the 1890s a road went off to the right here, north-eastwards. This was Upper Edmund Street, dissecting Suffolk Street (roughly on the line of present day Battle Bridge Road) and stretching as far as the entrance to the Imperial Gas Works (see p 89). The expansion of passenger facilities on this west side of the main terminus entailed the demolition of a number of residential streets, including Ashby, Northampton and Norfolk Streets, which had terraced housing dating from the 1850s. The suburban platforms were built in 1875 and extended westwards in 1895 by the reconstruction of this west wall and the construction of a new roof over all the platforms here.

Until the CTRL works are further advanced you may have to take the gated path indicated to the car park through to the car park's exit in Battle Bridge Road and thence to Culross Buildings. Otherwise continue and draw alongside the large building opposite, with the prominent tiled roof. This is the former **German Gymnasium**, built in 1864–5 by Edward A Grüning for the German Gymnastic

20 German Gymnasium in action (drawing, 1866). Note the climbing ropes hanging from roof trusses 77

Society along the lines of such institutions in Germany, where the gymnasium had been popularised by Ludwig Jahn in the early 19th century. It opened in January 1865, initially for Germans, though within a decade at least a half of its 1,100 members were English. Laminated timber arches supporting iron spandrels span the breadth of the hall, a construction used also for the original roofs of King's Cross Station. The gymnasium (Fig 20), the last of its kind to survive in England, was wound up in 1914. Sold to the GNR, the building was damaged during a daylight air raid in July 1917. Until recently it was used as a studio, but there are plans for it to house a ticket office for the new terminal.

Beyond the Gymnasium until recently were two short streets: Clarence Passage and Stanley Passage (known as Red Lion Passage until 1937). In the latter stood **Stanley Buildings**, one of the oldest surviving examples of working-class flats in London. One complete block and part of another have been saved from demolition.

The 5-storey blocks (of which there were originally five) were erected in 1864–5 by the Improved Industrial Dwellings Company, whose chairman was Lord Stanley (later Earl of Derby and Prime Minister). Designed by John Dower, and adapted from Henry Robert's model cottages for the Great Exhibition, the blocks have cast-iron access balconies served by an open central staircase. Here

Mike Leigh set his 1988 film *High Hopes*.

Beyond Stanley Buildings on this side of the road, the next right turning is **BATTLE BRIDGE ROAD**. It was formed in the early 1890s when the former Suffolk Street and its neighbouring streets were removed. Until WW I the road led into York Way, onto which face the buildings visible across the railway lines. **Culross Buildings** on the right were built in 1891–2 for the GNR as a replacement for dwellings it demolished. It is a rare survival of a tenement style of flats applied to railway housing. The windows and doors are now bricked up, but the flats used to be reached from open communal stairs with wrought-iron balustrades. There was a basement for railway workshops and messrooms, accessible only from the rear (by the railway tracks). At the end of the road is a car park formed in 2001 on the site of a former blacksmith's forge, and in the corner is **Culross Hall**, one of three mission halls the GNR erected along its route as centres for religious guidance and recreation.

Retrace your steps. On the northern side of the street a new road has been formed, leading into Goods Way through the site of the former Imperial Gas Works, demolished in 1921. It affords a view of the tall Granary building (p 82) in King's Cross Goods Yard, which we will inspect more closely later.

Back at **King's Cross Station**, walk

past the entrance to platforms 9–11 and bear right past a parcel-handling area, where on the wall there is a blue plaque to Sir Nigel Gresley (1876–1941), a locomotive engineer who had offices here; the loco *Mallard*, still holder of the world steam speed record, was among his designs.

Walk under the wrought-iron porte-cochère, built to protect passengers alighting from carriages. Formerly the station's main entrance, it faced on to the former wedge-shaped gardens in front of the Great Northern Hotel. Enter the station by the next entrance left, just opposite the hotel.

Pause to admire the train shed, whose ribs of wrought iron (which in 1866–67 replaced the original laminated timber) rise from dignified brick arcades. The departure and arrival sheds are spanned by two round arched roofs, each with a span of 105 ft, and cover an area 800 ft long, 210 ft wide and 72 ft high. When the station opened in 14 October 1852 it was the largest in Britain, but it soon was unable to cope with the amount of traffic. This increased further after 1857 when the GNR allowed the Midland Railway Company (MR) to run into the station, although it was frequently said that Midland trains were deliberately held back to give precedence to those of the GNR. The MR withdrew after its St Pancras station opened in 1868.

The station suffered bomb damage during WW II. On the morning of 11 May 1941 a heavy explosive bomb destroyed the western range of offices, but the blast also brought down four of the arched ribs, which were replaced after the war in a slightly different design from the originals.

Walk across to Platform 1 on the far side and turn along it. Continue, under an impressive clock on a decorated iron bracket, to the end of the train shed, with a cab road on your right. The Italianate tower in the distance is a remnant of the former Metropolitan Cattle Market. Note also the three tunnels beyond the platform end. The passage of trains beneath the Regent's Canal presented great problems. Cast-iron aqueducts were needed to carry the canal; limited clearances and steep gradients subjected steam trains to a fearsome climb out of London. The original two-track tunnel (with a semicircular portal) also became a serious bottleneck as traffic increased; it was supplemented by the now disused tunnel on the right in 1878, and by that on the left in 1892. The line leads straight out of Camden to re-emerge in Islington.

Before we leave King's Cross Station, it is worth dispelling some of the myths popularly associated with its site. Some say that Boudicca's remains after the battle of AD 61 are buried under Platform 10. Others hold that the ruins of Troynovant, Britain's mythological ancient capital, lie under the station. Here King Arthur would have drawn Excalibur from the stone. And a contemporary legend is also associated with the station: in J K Rowling's novels, Harry Potter's train to Hogwarts departs from Platform 9¾.

Now walk up the cobbled ramp, taking care to avoid the many black cabs that use it. By the entrance in **YORK WAY** look right; set into the brickwork of the outer wall is a rectangular St Pancras parish mark, dated 1853. We are standing by the former entrance to the York Road station, a single platform used by southbound trains running through to the City over the Metropolitan lines. Its opening on 1 June 1866 did little to alleviate the congestion at King's Cross or delays to trains waiting to enter the main station; it still took 30 minutes to travel the 1½ miles from Holloway. 'York Road' had its own booking office, removed after the station closed on 15 March 1977, when suburban trains to Moorgate were electrified and diverted via Essex Road.

York Way has had various names. The oldest road to the north in the parish, it was said by the historian William Camden to have existed by 1300. It appears to have been first called Longwich Lane, and was deep and dirty in winter. It was sometimes called Black Dog Lane, as it led to the Black Dog inn at Highgate. Passing middens or dust heaps, it became known as Midden Lane, later Maiden Lane, although Ambrose Heal records another tradition: that it was named after an image of the Virgin that stood beside the road before the Reformation. Maiden Lane, doubled in width, became York Road in the 1850s after the opening of the GNR (briefly known as the London & York). In 1938 York Road became York Way.

The land along this western side of York Way was until the 1840s held by St Bartholomew's Hospital, and was formerly known as Allensbury or, alternatively, Elm Friars or Alkichesbury. It was known by this last name in 1249–50 when a Visitation by the church recorded that it comprised 60 acres, a grange, a garden and 2 villeins; and that it had been demised by a deed c.1168–81 by William de Belmeis, canon of St Paul's, to Stephen Albus of the Priory of St Bartholomew's. In 1846 Bart's sold the land to the GNR for £50,000. Interestingly, discussion of the future of the goods yard site in the 1980s revealed that the hospital had a residual claim to repurchase the site at 19th-century prices should the land cease to be used for railway purposes.

By the early 19th century the land along Maiden Lane was cheap. Dickens wrote in *Our Mutual Friend* that the area was a semi-industrial twilight zone, "a tract of suburban Sahara, where tiles and bricks were burnt, bones were boiled, rubbish was shot, dogs fought and dust was heaped by contractors". A drawing of 1843 by

George Scharf shows carpet grounds, where carpets slung across large wooden posts were beaten by women wielding 6-ft poles. South of the canal the land taken by the GNR for the station and its approach had been developed in the first quarter of the 19th century. A number of little roads had been demolished: Union Place, (Lower) Edmund Street and part of Norfolk Street, as well as Stephenson Street (roughly where we are now).

Cross Goods Way. On the corner is a bell-shaped iron bollard intended to prevent the many local lorries from mounting the kerb. At the canal bridge pause to look left at the canal and the buildings of the Goods Yard. **Maiden Lane Bridge** was built in 1819. It was widened and rebuilt in 1852, in 1923, and most recently in 1998 to comply with EC legislation on minimum loading, but parts of the original fabric, including some fine cast-iron work, were retained. Stop gates were installed underneath during WW II to prevent flooding of the railway tunnel below by bombs: each night these gates were pulled shut. Note how the canal widens near the bridge – to the left, barges used to moor at the two Albion Flour Mills, which operated here from the mid-19th century until the late 1880s.

After the bridge turn left through the entrance to the former **Goods Yard**, marked North London Freight Depot, but actually Wharf Road. There is another bell bollard on the pavement.

The GNR's goods yard covered some 59 acres. It is strange to be able to enter it today, because goods yards were previously secret places, walled off from the outside world and guarded like naval dockyards. The yard is one of the most important of its kind, designed by Lewis Cubitt in 1850 as the largest goods station of the period. The GNR revolutionised the supply of key commodities into London, carried from the rich farmland along its route. It helped stimulate demand for agricultural produce by the speed and regularity of supply, which drove down costs and improved the quality of food on sale in London markets. Keen to wrest control of the coal trade to London from the sea-borne carriers, the GNR built coal-drops in the yard. The only thing now missing from the picture is the link to the Regent's Canal and thence to the Docks: originally, the yard contained two canal basins (filled in long ago) which enabled the smooth transfer of goods from railway to canal and vice versa.

The future of the yard hangs in the balance. In 1987 British Rail announced its intention to develop the site, linked to a plan for a low-level terminal of the Channel Tunnel Railway at King's Cross Station. Sir Norman Foster won a competition in 1988 with a design for an office city of 7.5 million square feet of office floor space, including two 44-storey towers, which was to be developed by the London Regeneration Consortium. The scheme was thwarted by recession and some very active local campaigning. A revised plan, including a massively enlarged terminus at St Pancras Station, was enshrined in the Channel Tunnel Rail Link Act of 1996 with certain safeguards for the local community. London and Continental Railways Ltd, the promoters, were declared bankrupt within two years but the Government brokered a rescue involving Railtrack. Their subsidiary Company is now responsible for building the new rail link and has been letting contracts for massive civil engineering works at St Pancras. The land here (north of the canal) is now owned by Exel plc, and the developers (Argent St George) still plan to convert the whole area into 'King's Cross Central' for office, retail, residential and urban entertainment uses. At the time of writing the development still looks a long way off – construction is not planned to begin until 2007, after the completion of the new terminal. This does mean, however, that for now this southern part of the Goods Yard still retains many of its facilities from the 1850s.

Continue left along the pavement. The open area across the road was the site of the temporary passenger terminus of 1850 that preceded King's Cross and was known as Maiden Lane station. It opened on 7 August 1850, and before its closure on 14 October 1852 had to cope with huge crowds coming to London for the Great Exhibition and with at least one royal departure for the North. Indeed at one time the GNR directors considered making it their permanent terminus, since crossing of the canal was such a major obstacle.

After the station had been abandoned it was converted in just 3 days into a wholesale potato market, which was successively enlarged and adapted. Potatoes from Yorkshire were one of the GNR's most important commodities, and the Potato Market (Fig 21) quickly became established as the leading one in London, with nearly 1,000 tons sold in a week in the mid-1860s. The GNR's yard was more convenient for traders than Covent Garden and the supply was always regular, unlike that of the sea carriers on whom the traditional centre at Tooley Street depended. The potato trade here reached a peak after WW I.

The southern part of the Potato Market was demolished in 1970. It is now used by a storage and distribution firm, who also make use of what looks like an old platform. The area is covered by a curved, gabled roof supported on trusses attached to brackets along the eastern wall of a large railway shed. The shed was first built as a carriage shed for the Maiden Lane terminus by GNR, who agreed in 1858 to its use for goods traffic by the MR, which shortly afterwards completed its own coal depot in Agar Town. It retained the name Midland Goods Shed but was altered in 1888 in response to the potato dealers' request that they be given better accommodation for their market. At the southern end of the shed there is

a 3-storey, 7-bay building, formerly offices but now very dilapidated.

A little further on is a 5-bay building, erected in 1850 as goods offices when purpose-built examples were rare; it had

21 Potato Market, 1864

large windows and a convenient plan. It was renovated in the late 1980s and renamed **Regeneration House**, as the site HQ of the London Regeneration Consortium. It now houses offices of Exel plc.

Beyond rises the imposing **Granary** building of 1852, sufficiently impressive for its architect Lewis Cubitt to display a watercolour of it at the Royal Academy. Six floors high, with a prominent cornice which hides a double-hipped roof, it has an internal frame of cast-iron columns and beams with timber joists and floor surfaces. The top floor originally contained large water tanks holding 150,000 gallons used in a low pressure hydraulic power system for operating hoists. Sacks could be transferred from the top to the ground floor by a series of chutes. The Granary is flanked by two 580-ft transit sheds designed for trans-shipment of goods between rail, road and canal, and containing stabling for the GNR's cart horses. Security officers prevent casual access to the buildings which are currently used by Pickfords, but since 1989 it has also been home to Raceway, Europe's longest (and widest) indoor karting circuit (750 metres) whose clients are allowed past. The track is open daily.

Continue past the inter-war concrete access bridge from Goods Way, which has recently acquired a new neighbour to the west. In the paving in front of the Granary note the outline of the original canal basin (now filled in) from which two short canal docks entered the building; when not in use the docks could be covered over.

We soon reach, to our left, a sombre collection of brick buildings. Just in front of the buildings there used to be a railway bridge which carried coal wagons to the Imperial Gas works opposite, but no trace of this remains. Alongside it was Somers Bridge, built in 1819, which provided access to the goods yard when it first opened and for nearly 90 years, until it was taken down and replaced by the concrete bridge we have already passed.

The buildings, former **Coal and Fish Offices**, were constructed in several phases from 1852. The words *Coal Office* can just be discerned, painted in white. The block was damaged by fire in 1983, but permission to demolish it was refused after a public inquiry in 1985. Walk past it, noting in front the old railway sleepers used to form flower boxes, and continue as the road bends to the right, following the line of the canal. Proceed until the pavement gives out at a metal barrier, and stop to survey the scene.

Over the brick wall to your left is the canal, and on its opposite bank are St Pancras Lock, the red-brick water point (p 91) above St Pancras Basin, and Camley Street Natural Park (p 91). The Natural Park is on the site of coal drops, built in 1865–67, which were reached by a bridge over the canal, now removed but featured in the movie *Alfie* (1966). The viaduct across the yard leading to the bridge survives, as do railway lines across the roadway. The large building ahead, with prominent old British Rail "Drive Slowly" signs, is the **Western Goods Shed**, built in 1897–9 on the site of the original coal and stone-handling basin. Offices were provided over the shed on this western side.

To the right of the Goods Shed are the **Western Coal Drops**, built in 1859–60, and converted for general goods transit when the Western Goods Shed was built. The Loading Bay canopy is supported by steel cantilevered beams and ornate cast-iron brackets; walk across for a closer view. Beyond the viaduct at the other side of the yard – now used by the brewers Charles Wells – are the **Eastern Coal Drops** built in 1851, which originally carried four high-level railway tracks from which wagons discharged coal into storage bins on a mezzanine floor above cart-loading bays. The distribution of coal from the north-east and Yorkshire was an important part of GNR's goods traffic, and when first built these drops were claimed to be capable of handling 1,000 tons a day. Later in the 19th century the southern section of the building was converted into a warehouse, which now houses film studios and **Bagley's** night club (named for Bagley's Bottle Warehouse), with space for over 2,000 people and host to numerous 'rave' music events. Potted palm trees grace the veranda.

Return along the roadway, but on the pavement opposite to the one we took earlier. Look left over the side; there is old stabling beneath. The stables here were partly ventilated by openings on the canal side, and could house 120 horses. It is estimated that by 1900 the GNR yard as a whole used 1,500 horses on deliveries. Far from reducing the need for horse labour, the railways increased it. There was even a horse infirmary in the north corner of the goods yard. Part of the stabling here has been converted to another night club, **The Cross**, its 'garden' swathed in greenery below us.

Continue back to York Way and turn left, preparing for a rather arduous 15-minute walk along a decidedly unattractive thoroughfare. (Alternatively, catch a bus to the corner of Agar Grove (p 84), noting the sights described below in a little more comfort.) Walk past the old Potato Market site, and crossing the busy main road, continue along the opposite (Islington) side. Having crossed Copenhagen Street, look back at two forlorn iron columns. These are the sole survivors of the roof that once covered the cobbled roadway between the market and York Way. Just beyond on this Islington side is the attractive Victorian frontage of York Way School, in a neo-Gothic style yet looking very new; the school was reopened in January 2001.

As York Way rises, look through the railings for an overall view of the northern part of the railway lands. Note in particular the large northern frontage of the transit sheds that flank The Granary. Nearer to us, but no longer standing, was the Hydraulic Accumulator Tower, evidence that hydraulic power was once very important in the operation of the yard. The tall posts are remains of a high fence that surrounded what was, until 2000, central London's only full-length golf driving range, laid out on former coal-stacking sidings. It now houses temporary buildings associated with the CTRL works.

Pass, on your right, the mulberry-tiled buildings of the abandoned York Road Underground station. Opened on 15 December 1906, it was one of three little-used Piccadilly Line stations closed in the 1930s. A fine example of the work of architect Leslie W Green, it was renovated in 1989.

Away to your left, on the far side of the present 'wasteland', were several large engine sheds, collectively known as 'Top Shed' (Fig 22, p 84). This was the place to see the LNER's express passenger locomotives, such as the famous *Flying Scotsman*. There, too, was the King's Cross Locomotive Works, where engines underwent both maintenance and major overhauls. The sheds were all demolished in 1963 at the close of the age of steam.

It is now a rather long walk up York Way to the edge of the railway lands, over what was once a viaduct across the great expanse of railway tracks fanning out into the Goods Yard. Shield your eyes, as the road becomes very dusty. This is because nearby is the northern entrance to the **Freight Terminal**, home not only to road haulage firms but also to waste disposal and a large cement works, marked out by three huge grey silos in the middle distance. Past the busy entrance is a bunker-like, brick and corrugated iron building which houses Camden Council offices.

Proceed under the bridge that carries the former North London Line (now used by Silverlink). A railway line from Camden Town to the docks at Blackwall had been authorised by an Act of Parliament in 1846, but the line first ran into Fenchurch Street and was able to build up what proved to be valuable passenger traffic. Opened to the Docks in 1852, and originally known as the East & West India Docks & Birmingham Junction Railway, it was able to compete successfully for goods traffic with the Regent's Canal – but it is best known as a commuters' line, the North London Railway. There was a passenger station here in Maiden Lane from 1887 until 1916, when it was hit by a bomb and never replaced. Its booking-office building of two storeys, just north of the bridge, was demolished in the 1970s.

Continue the climb up York Way. When we cross Vale Royal we are on the

22   The original King's Cross Locomotive Shed (drawing, c.1850). The crescent-shaped shed lay in the northern part of the Goods Yard

site of the ironically named Belle Isle, which in the 19th century was a collection of ramshackle industrial buildings with tall chimneys, devoted to bone boiling, blood boiling, carrion boiling, varnish making and the manufacture of artificial manure. Here, horses that had finished their useful working life were slaughtered. A leading article in *The Metropolitan* (13 September 1856) states that "the nuisance makers of Belle Isle are still permitted to affect their neighbours with nausea, sickness, diarrhoea, dysentery and cholera to any extent they please for their own private advantage". The St Pancras Vestry minutes record several petitions about the noxious odours from Belle Isle.

On the opposite side of the roadway were the coal depot and the cattle and sheep pens of the cattle depot of the LNWR (which here used North London line tracks). The pens had been relocated from Camden Town ready for the opening of the Caledonian Cattle Market (once off York Way, a little further up on the right). Imagine herds of cattle having been unloaded from trucks from Shropshire being driven to market at this spot! The new market was opened in June 1855 on the site of Copenhagen House and Fields, a favourite tea garden and meeting place of Londoners in the 18th century.

Continue, noting (opposite) the entrance to the Maiden Lane Estate, until the traffic lights are reached. Here we cross over to regain Camden territory at the end of a short row of tall 19th-century houses, now shops, with stucco window surrounds, originally known as New Market Terrace. On the corner with Agar Grove is the **Newmarket Ale House**, which was licensed as a theatre from 1867 to 1871, when it was called the New Market Inn. Its proprietor at that time was Charles Buckhurst, who owned the pub, the stables and sheds behind and a long triangular portion of land, on which in 1876 he opened a roller-skating rink (see below).

Turn left along **AGAR GROVE**, as St Paul's Road was renamed in 1938. We have now crossed over the boundary of St Pancras Manor, here Allensbury. The actual boundary ran behind the gardens of the houses on this south side. The houses on both sides of the road belong to the more northerly Camden Square development, which began at the far (western) end of St Paul's Road in 1846 and was largely complete by 1860.

St Paul's Road originally enjoyed a good reputation, its inhabitants featuring in the Court Guides. At **No.87**, opposite, lived Augustine Aglio (1836–75), a landscape painter like his father, the more famous Agostino Aglio (d.1857). By the 1890s, however, most of the houses were let out as apartments and lodgings, and by the Edwardian period the road shared with much of Camden Town a distinctly demi-monde reputation, reinforced by the murder of Phyllis Dimmock at No.29 (see p 86).

Take the first left turn into **ST PAUL'S CRESCENT**, which when first built was known as St Paul's Terrace. At No.37 the pioneer of silent films Cecil Hepworth lived when an infant. The street begins with charming mid-19th-century cottages (2 storeys plus basement) on both sides. On the left we soon come to the gated and very private development of **St Paul's Mews**, designed by the CZWG Partnership, in 1987–91. One can peer through to glimpse the double-curving sweep of town houses whose construction caused something of an outcry in 1987 because of a perceived lack of consultation.

Camden Skating Rink, an indoor roller-skating rink, was here from 1876 to 1900, at which date Joseph Thornley (who had lived at No.122 St Paul's Road) ceased to be the ratepayer. He had been the proprietor for 20 years and had given

a deposition at the inquest in August 1890 of 15-year-old Charles George who had collapsed and died at the rink (verdict "syncope whilst suffering from heart disease"). The rink became a builders' yard in the 20th century.

Cross to the turning opposite. Walk into a yard full of ramshackle workshops awaiting restoration and mostly dating from the late 19th century, when this was a waterproofing works; the ARC lamps lighting company had works here from 1900. The building to the left with its barge-boarded gabled entrance is shown on the 1870 OS map as a house in its own park-like grounds.

Returning to the street and turning right, we reach the decidedly run-down **Maiden Lane Estate**. This was begun in 1976 and finished by 1983, on the site of the coal and cattle depots of the LNWR. The first tenants moved in in 1980, but after only a few months there were many complaints about design faults and constructional failings (for example, dust carts could not get into the estate, and drainage was inadequate on the stepped houses). Designed by Gordon Benson and Alan Forsyth, who were also responsible for the redevelopment of Gospel Oak, the estate is mainly low-rise with west-facing terraces above garages.

At the end of the street ahead is the **Maiden Lane Community Centre**, which includes a squash court and gym and

hosts a playgroup and a youth club. Do not make for this but turn immediately left up the red-brick path, ignoring **Rosebank Walk** and the steps leading up to **Linkwood Walk**, and turn right into present-day **MAIDEN LANE**. The name of this tiny crescent, which does not lie on the line of the long thoroughfare now called York Way, recalls the history of the area, as do those of **Allensbury Place**, **Broadfield Lane** and **Elm Friars Walk**. The clock tower of St Pancras Chambers is clearly visible beyond the grassy mound at the end of the street, for which we aim. At the end, walk up the steps to the right, turning right at the top and then immediately left along a passageway passing front doors. Here there are good views, right, over the estate. The passage opens out, past a grassy area, into a patio that affords a splendid panorama over the railway lands towards central London. Prominent are the silos of the cement works and beyond the train sheds of both King's Cross and St Pancras Stations.

Continue to the end of the patio, where there is a ramp leading down between white concrete walls. Walk down the ramp, proceed to the trees planted in the paved area ahead and then turn left down steps (the pathway is called **ST JAMES GATE**) and continue, with a fenced-in playground away to your left. Beyond this turn right, by the side of the main railway line to the East Midlands. Shortly after the line opened, a temporary chapel occupied the ground where trees now stand. It was used in the 1870s as a branch of the Free Christian Church, whose headquarters was in Clarence Road, Kentish Town, and where "all seat holders are members and no doctrinal test whatever can be imposed". The minister of the chapel here in 1874 was Moncure Conway, at the time also pastor of South Place Unitarian Chapel, Finsbury, and who is remembered in Conway Hall, Red Lion Square, the present home of the South Place Ethical Society. The temporary chapel was later used by Wesleyans before its site was taken over by the MR.

The railway line obliterated Queen's Road, a turning off St Paul's Road which stretched as far as the North London Line, but which was projected to connect up with King's Road (p 87) across northern Agar Town. In the 1850s, when Queen's Road and the two streets off it (Wrotham and Elm Roads) were developed, the area here was known as Agar New Town. Its first houses appear to have been built in 1852. No.1 Queen's Road contained the Camden Congregational Chapel.

Walk past the white painted wall. This follows the ancient boundary of St Pancras Prebendal Manor and formed the boundary of the former coal and cattle depot. Behind it are the workshops we saw off St Paul's Crescent. Regain **AGAR GROVE** and look right. Diagonally

opposite, the second house along is **No.29**, where Emily 'Phyllis' Dimmock was murdered. On 11 September 1907 she was found dead in her bed, her throat "cut almost from ear to ear". In lodgings here she had lived a double life: by day she was the devoted common-law wife of Bert Shaw, a Midland Railway restaurant-car cook; by night, while Bert worked a night shift on trains to Sheffield, she continued her former career as a prostitute, touting for trade in local pubs. Among her favourite haunts was the Rising Sun in Euston Road (p 41). The Old Bailey trial of Robert Wood, an outwardly respectable designer of glassware patterns, was a *cause célèbre*, as the first murder trial in which the defendant gave testimony from the witness box. The case caught the public imagination of an underworld of sleazy, decaying houses, with lodging houses used for prostitution. It also inspired Walter Sickert to paint his 'murder series'.

Turn left. Opposite is the old Agar Grove coal depot. On the next corner is the **Murray** pub, dating from the late 1840s. A few steps to the left beyond the pub, turn right into cobbled **COBHAM MEWS**. This turning is now home to a pair of 2-storey studio offices by David Chipperfield architects (1990), with a "forceful shared formal entrance" (Cherry & Pevsner), each with an extension expanding into the limited space available.

Go back to Agar Grove and cross over

left into the **Agar Grove Estate**. This was completed in 1969, on the site of Elm Road and most of Wrotham Road. The street down which we turn was laid out in 1865 alongside the railway line, replacing the demolished Queen's Road. It was initially called Wrotham Villas, then Lomond Street from 1871 until 1886, when it was renamed as a continuation of Wrotham Road. Walk past Ujima Housing Association flats erected in 2000, rich in stained wood. Then turn right towards the centrepiece of the estate, the tower block of flats called **Lulworth**. Built in 1965, the tower block had an unenviable reputation for crime until the tenants took over its management in December 1996.

It covers the site of No.30 St Paul's Road, a large detached house built in the 1840s as The Lodge, and set back from the roadway, abutting the Agars' land. The Lodge was the home in 1871 of George Cruikshank, a watercolour artist, almost certainly related to his more famous artist namesake who died in 1878 at No.263 Hampstead Road. A near neighbour (at No.34a) was Frederick Selby Meakin, an architect in partnership with his father, William Fountain Meakin.

By the tower block, look left at **Agar Grove Community Nursery**, opened in 1993, and standing on the site of St Thomas', Wrotham Road. St Thomas' was built in 1862–3 partly out of the funds (£6,000) supplied by the MR for the erection of a church, school and parsonage to replace a church in Agar Town then being torn down. The replacement, by S S Teulon (1812–73), the architect of St Stephen's, Hampstead, had diapered brickwork, a pyramidal roof and an unusually large unsupported span. Pevsner described it as "immensely coarse". In 1948 the benefice was placed under the charge of the Vicar of St Michael, Camden Town and the two parishes were united in 1954. By then derelict, St Thomas' was pulled down and the site was sold in 1955. In front of the church was a towering 50-ft sycamore, known locally as the Ghost Tree of St Pancras, under which many newlyweds were photographed. The tree mysteriously died when plans to develop the area as a council estate were made public.

In Elm Road (also covered by the estate) was the vicarage of St Thomas'. At No.3, next door, lived the architect Henry George Luff (1843–1905), having been forced to move from his home in the demolished Queen's Road. A fellow architect, Henry John Wadling (1844–1918), pupil and assistant of James Piers St Aubyn, boarded with him.

Now turn right, and regain Agar Grove by turning left through the metal gate ahead. Nos.5&7, opposite, are a pair of 1840s villas, sporting a full entablature and Ionic pilasters. Here on the south side we reach a short road with a row of late-19th-century terraced artisan houses. This is

AGAR PLACE. The same name is now applied to the turning on the opposite side of Agar Grove. Now a cul-de-sac, this once ran into Camden Road and was first called Camden Cottages Mews (subsequently Rochester Place); it is shown as such on the 1827 Greenwood map, and is thus one of the oldest side roads in this vicinity. Turn left along cobbled Agar Place. At the end, turn right to walk down all that is left of **WROTHAM ROAD** – just two mid-19th-century stuccoed houses with central doorways, facing three later-19th-century terraced houses with polychrome brick surrounds to the windows.

At the corner of **ST PANCRAS WAY** is a pair of fine mid-19th-century stuccoed villas. St Pancras Way was formerly King's Road. In this area was the original St Pancras Workhouse, opened in 1731, and shown as a ruin in James King's Kentish Town Panorama, the exact location being unclear. In 1772 the workhouse building was declared unsafe and the Vestry subsequently took over The Mother Black Cap (then on the site of Camden Town Underground station), although the inmates did not move in until 1778. This second building soon became overcrowded and the workhouse moved again in 1809 to new purpose-built accommodation, now St Pancras Hospital (p 97), at the southern end of King's Road.

The ruins shown in King's drawing may include the remnants not only of the first workhouse, but also of the house in which William Bruges, first Garter King of Arms, lived in the 15th century, and in which he entertained the Holy Roman Emperor, Sigismund, in lavish style in 1416. Bruges' house could well have been built as near as possible to the most important house in St Pancras manor, the manor house, which was nearby.

Also very near here is the conjectured site of the medieval manor house of Cantelowes Manor, roughly where the row of early-19th-century terraced houses stand, on the opposite side of St Pancras Way. This terrace, shown on the 1827 map as Brecknock Terrace, was matched by another terrace opposite, to our left (and now demolished), known as St Paul's Terrace, its name presumably derived from the centuries-old connection between St Pancras and St Paul's Cathedral.

The walk ends here. It is a short walk along Baynes Street opposite beneath the railway, turning right and then left to Camden Road, where there is the Silverlink railway station and, further along, Camden Town Underground station. Those who wish to do so can walk all the way back towards King's Cross by turning left along St Pancras Way, under the railway bridge, to the corner of Barker Drive, and then following Route 6 (from p 95).

Through lost Agar Town

Leave King's Cross Underground station by the exit marked "Pancras Road, British Library" and at the end, turn left up the steps and then sharp right into **PANCRAS ROAD**.

Pancras Road was originally part of medieval Gray's Inn Lane, which ran north from Holborn. Having crossed the River Fleet at Battle Bridge, it ran west, then northwest towards Kentish Town. When St Pancras Station was built, Pancras Road was straightened, to follow the side of the station to a right-angled junction with Euston Road. The curving wall of the Great Northern Hotel reveals the original alignment of the road.

Here, on its west side, was Weston Place, small houses developed in the 1790s by William Weston, who was receiving a tidy £27 per annum in rent for each by 1814. In that year the religious fanatic Joanna Southcott (Fig 23), having lived for many years at No.17, died of a brain tumour. She claimed shortly before her death that she was pregnant with a second Prince of Peace, miraculously conceived, she being in her sixties at the time. In its last days, before its demolition in 1871,

Weston Place had numerous pubs and coffee houses to cater for travellers arriving at King's Cross Station.

Weston Place abutted the southern end of the estate of the Brewers' Company,

23   The religious fanatic Joanna Southcott (c.1750–1814)

who obtained an Act of Parliament in 1811 to pave and improve it. This led to the removal of a tile kiln (here since at least 1752) and to the growth of streets that were all later demolished to make way for

St Pancras station: Weston Street, Smith Street, Denton Street and Perry Street. Weston House in Weston Street, a building of some pretension, was advertised as an establishment for insane ladies in 1837 and later called "Penitent Female Asylum" before it moved to 200 Euston Road.

Pancras Road was known by the 19th century as Old St Pancras Road, progressively assuming its present unsainted name in 1872–81. Long since confined in an iron conduit, the River Fleet once flowed here along its west side. Samuel Bagster (p 45) remembered it as having been (c.1760) "a clear ever-flowing rivulet of five or six feet wide and about a foot deep, unless when swollen by long continued rain". This stretch of the road on the low-lying plain to the south of St Pancras Old Church was prone to serious flooding, earning the area the name Pancras Wash. In 1809 and again in 1818 the whole area between the Church and Battle Bridge (King's Cross) was covered with water 3 ft deep.

Walk up Pancras Road, by the richly decorated side wall of St Pancras station, and admire details such as the undercut capitals and the lions' heads terminating the drip moulds above the arcading of the archways. On most days bric-a-brac spills out onto the pavement, although the shops here are due to close when work on extending St Pancras Station to receive the new Channel Tunnel Rail Link (CTRL) is fully underway. Every so often you can peer into the entrances to the cavernous vaults below the station, whose platforms were raised well above ground level to allow the tracks to cross over the canal just north of the station. The cellars below once housed beer barrels but are now mainly occupied by car valeting firms, and are due to become ticket halls and shops for the CTRL terminus.

The CTRL works have diverted the course of Pancras Road to bend towards the side of King's Cross Station, to which we walk, then continue past the German Gymnasium (p 77), Stanley Buildings and on the right the entrance to Battle Bridge Road (described in detail on pages 77–78). (Until the CTRL works are further advanced you may have to take the gated path indicated to the car park through to the car park's exit in Battle Bridge Road.)

Reach the junction with **GOODS WAY**. This western section was during the 19th century called Wharf Road and used to cross the Regent's Canal (which runs behind the wall on the opposite side, right) by the former Somers Bridge, built in 1819 and removed in WW II. The road was renamed in 1921 when the later eastern section was laid out on the site of the Imperial Gas Light & Coke Company's retort houses and extended to York Road, now York Way. Goods Way had a particularly seedy night-time reputation

in more recent years when it was notorious for kerb crawlers, including the then Director of Public Prosecutions, Sir Allen Green!

The Imperial Gas Light & Coke Company, formed in 1822, began a new works beside the canal. A short branch canal was opened in August 1824, and in the following year a large wharf was developed. Coal was discharged by crane and grab, operating from a gantry extending across the canal. A huge explosion in 1826 destroyed the steam engine house and was heard up to 4 miles away. In 1828 the company were found to be guilty of illegally extracting large quantities of water from the canal through pipes laid below the surface. The company ceased to manufacture gas here in 1904; by then there were nine gasometers on the site. The surrounding gasworks buildings were demolished in 1921.

The gasometers remained in use until 1999 and once formed a dramatic group (Fig 24), but now all but one have been removed. Three dating from the 1880s were Listed Grade II and have been stored for future re-siting by English Heritage, alongside the lone survivor to our right.

Cross Goods Way and continue along **CAMLEY STREET**. There is a good view back towards the shed and clock tower of St Pancras Station. Renamed n 1937, Camley Street was formerly Cambridge Street. This was the central

thoroughfare of **Agar Town**, an area developed by working men from 1840 onwards on small plots on 21-year leases offered by the widow of the landowner William Agar (p 92). The traditional view of Agar Town is that it was a squalid slum, housing many poor Irish who had been squeezed out of more central districts such as St Giles. Much of this stems from an influential article in Dickens' *Household Words* which depicted Agar Town as a suburban Irish shanty town. A different picture emerges from a study of records such as deeds, the Vestry minutes, the census and poor law records, and the interested reader is referred to CHS Occasional Paper 1: *Agar Town: The Life and Death of A Victorian 'Slum'.*

Some of the first buildings of Agar Town were built on the land to our left. The cottages appear to have been built by working men in their spare time, especially on Sundays, on leased plots typically 32 by 72 ft. Like most of Agar Town the small streets here remained unpaved and unlit until the late 1850s. In early 1860 the Imperial Gas Company bought out these lessees cheaply, cleared the site and constructed gas tanks – now themselves removed.

Agar Town's poor image meant that it fell easy prey to the Midland Railway (MR) Company, who obtained Parliamentary powers and swiftly demolished the area in 1866 in building their line into the new

St Pancras station, leaving the inhabitants to find other accommodation wherever they could. The MR's metropolitan extensions in the 1860s demolished 4,000 houses in Somers, Camden and Agar Towns, displacing perhaps as many as 32,000 people.

Along Cambridge Street were constructed coal drops or 'shoots' of both the MR (to our left, on the west side of the street) and the Great Northern Railway or GNR (on this side). The latter were the brainchild of Samuel Plimsoll (1824–98; p 62), a coal merchant who became more famous for his 'Plimsoll Line' to help the safety of merchant shipping (as well as to deter it from undercutting his railway interests by deliberate overloading). He had patented a coal drop that minimised the level of breakages, which was first successfully tried out within the GNR goods yard on the opposite bank of the canal (away to our right). The goods yard's boundaries were extended in 1865 when houses, stables and canal-side wharves fronting Cambridge Street were cleared and Plimsoll built a viaduct on iron girders across the canal. Below the railway line a series of bays was opened by 1868 for

24 Listed Gasometers in Camley Street (photo, Nov. 2001, from Goods Way) taken shortly before they were dismantled. The buildings in the foreground (on the site of former GNR stables) were the offices, since demolished, of Haden Young.

rental by different coal merchants. Wagons were pulled over the proper bay by a capstan and their contents were tipped down a chute for bagging up in the bay below, then loaded onto a cart and taken off for distribution.

With the post-WW II decline in the demand for coal, the two coal shoots were shut down, and in the 1960s demolished. The former MR coal shoot became a municipal rubbish tip. The site of the GNR coal drops was also used as a tip, although unofficially, and largely colonised by wild flowers. The Greater London Council eventually stepped in. After discarding plans for a coach park on the site it began the creation of **Camley Street Natural Park** in 1983. The Park opened in 1985, as a London Wildlife Trust nature reserve. On its first anniversary Ken Livingstone, then Leader of the GLC, inaugurated its fine wrought-iron gates, which had formerly stood at the MR goods depot in Somers Town (p 43).

Take time to explore the Natural Park (open every day except Friday), a two-acre wildlife haven with a Visitor Centre and year-round activities. It contains a pond, a view over the canal and a man-made hill with shaded bark-strewn walks. A seat by the pond can seem an oasis of calm, despite all the CTRL works close by.

Leave the Natural Park and turn right, past the gates of St Pancras Cruising Club. On the railway bank above the Club is the Listed water point of 1867, which was moved here in December 2001 from its earlier position by the railway bridge in Goods Way. It was originally built as a water tank to serve steam engines just outside St Pancras station. It has fine Gothic detailing: note the red and white patterning on its arches.

Cambridge Street originally continued straight on, but when the railway line was built the road was diverted underneath it. Present-day Camley Street, after swinging round underneath the railway line, resumes the original line of Cambridge Street over the canal and into what had been the MR's goods yard in northern Agar Town. The bending course of the road under the railway bridge more or less follows what was Cambridge Crescent, Agar Town. The Crescent was singled out for particular opprobrium in the 1851 *Household Words* article, which described it as "a few wretched hovels ranged in a slight curve, with huts of all shapes and sizes, full of costermongers". The 1851 census, however, shows that most of the single-family occupancy houses were headed by bricklayers or bricklayers' labourers. On the southern corner of Cambridge Street and Cambridge Crescent (just before the present railway bridge, opposite) an iron chapel, later faced in brick, opened in 1847 and survived until the demolition of the area in the 1860s. Facing it (before the bridge on this side of the footpath) was a public house called the Talbot Arms, named after William Agar's son, William Talbot Agar, whose mother was related to the Talbot Earls of Shrewsbury.

Walk under the three adjoining bridges. The farthest one is the oldest, constructed at Park Gate Steel Works, Rotherham in 1868, to carry the MR line into St Pancras. Just beyond it on the left, opposite, are the gates into St Pancras Gardens and St Pancras Coroner's Court (p 99).

Ascend the road as it bends to the right, noticing as we climb on the right-hand side of the road a number of old granite kerbstones laid on edge, somewhat sculpturally, as bollards. Interestingly, there was a stoneyard here in Agar Town. On the opposite side of the street were stables and railway offices at the entrance to the MR Goods Yard, now Parceline offices. Reach the **Oblique Bridge**, a concrete and steel replica, dating from the mid 1980s, of the original cast-iron structure. The bridge was first built in c.1820 (as Skew Bridge), to carry a driveway to Elm Lodge, the residence of William Agar. This northern part of Camley Street was laid out in the 1970s, after the Goods Yard closed. Further along the street, beyond the brick buildings, former railway offices, on the left, is residential Elm Village (p 93) and on the right "Camden's showpiece industrial estate", **CEDAR WAY**. The tower block in the distance is Lulworth on the Agar Grove Estate (p 86).

At the bridge, cross over and walk down the steps, left, and turn left under Oblique Bridge along the canal towpath. The canal narrows here so that a pair of stop gates could be closed if a section of canal needed to be drained. The **Regent's Canal** was opened on 1 August 1820, but its construction had been delayed by the actions of the local landowner, William Agar (1767–1838). Agar was a lawyer in the Court of Chancery (Fig 25). Called to the Bar in 1791 he was later made a King's Counsellor (KC) and is often referred to as Counsellor, or more confusingly Councillor, Agar. He had purchased the St Pancras estate of some 70 acres at auction in 1810 and for many years fought a battle – which at times literally came to blows – against the Regent's Canal Company to prevent his land being used for the canal. He had petitioned unsuccessfully against the Canal Bill in 1812 but after several court actions in 1818 he received compensation totalling over £15,000. Agar continued to complain and it was not until 1832 that matters were finally settled after 20 years of litigation.

At first the Regent's Canal was a vibrant artery of commerce, bringing trade and industry to the area. But the canal was to lose traffic to the railways and later to road transport. The last horse towed a barge along the canal in 1956. Now it is given over mainly to pleasure craft,

and walkers along the towpath; Camden opened its path in 1974, the year that the Regent's Canal was declared a Conservation Area

After passing under the railway bridges,

25   William Agar KC (drawing, date unknown)

observe to the right the expanse of **St Pancras Basin**. This was excavated in 1867 and opened in 1870 as a coal wharf for the MR. It was used for unloading ash from their locomotives into barges, which were taken up the canal to tips at Cowley

(near Uxbridge). Iron girders projecting from the west wall of the basin are the remnants of the coal staithes which used to run above the basin. It was reopened on 6 October 1958 as the St Pancras Basin, to provide moorings for 60 pleasure craft. In July 1961 the St Pancras Yacht Club was founded and the basin was fitted out for its use. It is now the St Pancras Yacht Basin, private HQ of the cruising club. The basin is overlooked by the red-brick water point (p 91).

Beyond the basin we reach **St Pancras Lock**. The first lock-keeper's cottage was on the site of the bench on this side, where you might care to rest to the sound of running water. The present lock-keeper's cottage opposite was built in 1898 as a pumping station to return water to the head of the lock.

Walk past the lock as far as the point where the towpath dips. Below the metal grilles on which we stand is the entrance to a canal basin which was built under the goods sheds of the GNR (left) to enable the transhipment of goods under cover. On the other bank of the canal is Camley Street Natural Park.

Now retrace your steps to the Oblique Bridge and continue along the towpath. We are walking beside an ivy-covered wall which once surrounded the former MR goods yard, opened in stages from 1862 to 1865. The MR here destroyed the northern and more select part of Agar Town, whose neat rows of terraces (such as Durham Street and Bolton Street) had been built less than a decade before, as well as building over the grounds of Elm Lodge. From the late 1880s the goods shed in the yard dealt mostly with incoming goods, arriving by rail from the north. Other facilities included a coal depot. During WW II the main goods shed was severely damaged by bombing but after repair it continued in use until the 1960s. The goods yard in its turn has been redeveloped and is now the Elm Village estate.

To our left, on the opposite side of the canal, the faceless, brown-panelled building was put up in 1980–1 by the Post Office as its Royal Mail North West District office, replacing its cramped sorting office in Eversholt Street (p 73). This had been the site of a huge warehouse known as The Granary (not to be confused with its more famous namesake in the GNR's goods yard), built in 1865 to house 100,000 barrels at a time of Bass Ale from Burton-on-Trent. Trade was less good than expected, and the warehouse was soon being used to store grain. From 1920 Woolworth's used it as its London depot. The Granary burned down in 1978 in a massive fire in which one fireman died. Rupert Murdoch bid unsuccessfully in 1979 to develop the 3-acre site as the base for News International, which subsequently moved to Wapping.

On this stretch of the canal there were once, in close proximity, two bridges. Pancras Bridge (Fig 26, p 94) was erected when the canal was constructed in 1819 and later carried Oxford Street, one of Agar Town's main thoroughfares. The New Bridge was put up in the 1850s to carry a road to link up with the Camden Square development via Queen's Road (p 86). Both bridges were demolished when the MR goods yard was laid out alongside the canal in the 1860s. To operate cranes and capstans in the yard a hydraulic pumping station was then constructed to house the steam engines that pumped water at pressure into a mains system. We now pass its ivy-covered remains, above which is the Jubilee Watersports Centre (entered from Crofters Way, Elm Village.) A little further on, at the bend in the canal, yet another bridge was constructed by the MR to carry a railway line over to sidings across the water to the warehouse when beer was delivered from the Midlands. Its pad stones are still visible on the wall.

We next encounter a small inlet, which contains a horse ramp. These ramps were built near railway bridges to lead horses out of the water if they fell in. Horses tended to bolt from the sudden noise of railway engines. The sloping path of the ramp can be seen by edging stone No.94. The number, incidentally, indicates a competitor's position during fishing competitions.

Beyond a wooden structure is a concrete balcony with prominently incised lettering reading "Elm Village 1983". We will visit the estate shortly.

Reach the road bridge carrying St Pancras Way and walk up the steps. Cross the road to the **Constitution** pub. This could be said to be the last remnant of Agar Town, a survivor of the few buildings which the MR left standing along the east side of what was then King's Road. It was built by the developer Thomas Bolton (who gave his name to Bolton Street, Agar Town) on a plot of land on which he had taken a 99-year lease from 5 March 1853.

Walk left towards the railway bridge (of the old North London line). The large building with a sloping wall, next to the bridge, was built by the MR in the 1880s for a customer, George Skey & Co., brick, pipe and tile maker of Wilnecote (Staffordshire); it housed 3-storey stables. The water tank served locomotives on the adjacent railway line. The building is now home to the **Camden Garden Centre**, which moved here from Kentish Town in 1990. All the Centre's profits are donated to a charitable trust which helps to employ, educate and train disadvantaged people.

Turn right before the Garden Centre into **Elm Village**, built on the old MR Goods Yard. The goods yard came into the possession of the London Borough of Camden in the 1970s, and in September 1975 the Council gave approval for 6 acres to form the new Elm Village, intended to house nearly 3,000 residents of the borough. These early plans came to naught, and complaints of vandalism and fly-tipping in the area were published. In 1980 the Department of Environment refused a loan sanction for council housing. Much of the site was subsequently sold for a mixed development of housing association and private housing named Elm Village, whose name recalls Agar's house Elm Lodge and its grounds, which once covered the site.

Walk up **BARKER DRIVE** and take the first turning on the right,

26 Pancras Bridge (drawing by Henry Guest RA, 1850s). In the background, St Pancras Workhouse

ROSSENDALE WAY. Note on the house opposite a blue plaque recording the Golden Jubilee Award from the Housing Centre Trust in 1984 to Elm Village for outstanding housing achievement. The Estate is certainly leafy and secluded and has a delightful homely charm. The brick and rendered surfaces are deceptive; timber framing allowed for speedy construction. From here look ahead to white stuccoed terrace houses in a style different from those surrounding us.

Walk towards these along **BERGHOLT MEWS**, with its Soane-like surrounds to the doors, until you reach a semicircular lawn in front of the terrace. Now turn left into **BLAKENEY CLOSE** and left again along a footpath, immediately in front of the houses, leading into a tiny triangular playground. This is more or less the site of Elm Lodge.

William Agar (p 92) built Elm Lodge for himself and his wife Louisa, niece of the Earl of Shrewsbury, after he purchased the estate in 1810. Drawings of the house (Fig 27, p 96) confirm that this was a late Georgian building, surrounded by a lawn, an orchard and a park full of mulberry trees. It was built on or near the site of the medieval St Pancras Manor House. The Agars' daughter Louisa was still living here in 1861, but the family had sold its interest in the estate the previous year and by 1862 the house was encircled by the MR Goods Yard. It was subsequently demolished by the MR after being used as railway offices into the 1880s.

Leaving the playground, return to Bergholt Mews. Its name has a rural feel, as do others on the Estate that we shall not visit (**Weavers Way, Ploughman's Close, Crofters Way** and **Reapers Close**). Turn right and out of the estate, turning left into **ST PANCRAS WAY**.

Until the late 18th century St Pancras Way was a continuation of Gray's Inn Lane leading from Holborn to Kentish Town. It later became known as King's Road, until 1938 when it was given its present name. Its winding route still follows the ancient track that ran alongside the River Fleet. The river is still here, but now enclosed in a storm-relief drain below ground.

Past the Constitution cross on to the canal bridge, with a view over Elm Village. The current 'Gray's Inn Bridge' was opened in 1897 by William Henry Matthews, Chairman of the Vestry, as the foundation plaque with a representation of St Pancras attests. Until the 1980s the bridge was a cast-iron structure, but it has been modernised; the iron panels have been lost but a view of canal has been opened up.

On the opposite side of the street, the long brick wall marks the site of a refuse destructor plant and subsequently the St Pancras Borough Electricity & Public Lighting Department's electricity generating station, which opened here in 1894, in response to strong public demand for electricity. It was supplied with water from the canal until the 1930s. It was closed in 1968.

On this side we are now walking alongside the boundary of what was Agar's property. In King's *Kentish Town Panorama* an immense row of poplars extended from here to Cook's Row (just beyond the present St Pancras Hospital). These are shown on Britton's parish map of 1834 but were cut down in 1840 when the first houses of Agar Town were built here, called Agar Cottages on the 1841 census.

Wharves were constructed along the canal and by the mid-19th century there were numerous goods yards and semi-industrial concerns along King's Road. For example, in the 1870s and 1880s on the west (opposite) side was H Schweitzer and Co., manufacturers of cocoatina, "the highest class of soluble cocoa or chocolate", and a firm of organ builders; the east (canal side) had a macaroni manufacturer and coal and lime wharves.

At the corner of Pratt Street (the second turning opposite) on the site of the post-modern flats at **No.49**, stood a fire station from 1888 until the 1940s. The large yard behind it was subsequently used as a Royal Mail depot. It is now the London Central Office of Parcel Force.

On this side, walk past a selection of office blocks of various shapes and sizes, including **Superchrome House**, one of a pair of moulded corrugated iron buildings. Reach the front of the former Post Office building (which we viewed from the canal) and on the pavement admire a VR post box in a style devised by the writer Anthony Trollope, still in use. The building has been renovated and houses offices. A hoarding a little further along carries a large picture of a lobster with a door through it. Until recently it also referred to the structure behind it, with a good deal of truth, as "The Ugly Brown Building".

Across the street a small turning known

27 Elm Lodge (drawing by Henry Guest RA, 1850s)

as **COLLEGE GROVE** was once a country lane which sloped down steeply to the River Fleet – there were two little bridges here on an 1825 map. It now leads past modern student accommodation, skirting the corner of a huge builders merchant's yard, which once housed the stables of the MR. Beyond the far end of the yard on St Pancras Way is a detached mid-Victorian house, **No.9**, which became a night shelter in 1974, and is now a St Mungo's hostel for older heavy drinkers.

To reach the front of the hostel cross **GRANARY STREET**. Initially Oxford Row, Agar Town, the road was renamed Cambridge Street after that street's course had been diverted by the MR's railway developments in the 1860s. After the Goods Yard closed down in the 1970s Cambridge Street (by now Camley Street) was extended along its original course, and this unprepossessing street was named after the huge warehouse that stood on its northern side until 1978. Much earlier, this was part of George Field, named from the George and Falcon, an inn on the opposite side of St Pancras Way, which was run by a Thomas George in 1693. The inn was subsequently renamed the Elephant and Castle after the supposed discovery of an elephant tusk in the River Fleet here in 1714. It has been claimed that the Danish fleet navigated the Fleet to this point in the 10th century. All that can be said with certainty is that the river bed was then much lower. The name may alternatively refer to the arms of the Cutlers' Company, a local landowner. The Elephant & Castle was licensed as a theatre from 1854–91 and remained in business until WW I, when it was used as the HQ of the National Reserve (St Pancras Battalion).

The inn was almost directly opposite the entrance to **St Pancras University Hospital and Hospital for Tropical Diseases**, which we now reach. The hospital was built on George Field in 1809 as the parish workhouse. Much enlarged in the 19th century – in 1911 it housed 1,200 people – the former workhouse is now run by the Camden and Islington Community Health Services Trust as a hospital for elderly patients.

By the corner of Pancras Road (p 98) one can view the hospital grounds, with willow trees and benches, and the hospital chapel. Alongside it is the site of the sometime St Pancras Town Hall, first built as the Vestry Hall. The Vestry had met at various taverns until the Hall was erected in 1847 to designs by its surveyor, Mr Bond, who forgot to include stairs to the first floor and had to add ugly steps outside. A new Vestry Hall (later St Pancras Town Hall) by architect H H Bridgman opened in April 1875, to be superseded by the Town Hall in Euston Road in 1937. George Bernard Shaw attended Vestry meetings here.

In early Victorian times the poor seeking outdoor relief had to wait outside the Vestry Hall without shelter from the early hours of the morning until they were seen. Up to 900 people might gather, and it could be 8 pm before relief was given, in the 'Black Hole', a room below the hall, with foul air and disgusting conditions. The St Pancras Vestry shared the then widely held utilitarian belief that poverty was immoral.

A few steps further on was once a row of late-18th-century terraced houses called Cook's Row, shown in King's panorama as built by a Captain Cook of Hampstead, although it seems that a Somers Town butcher called Cook leased the ground. They first appear on Thompson's parish map of 1804. They were replaced by the St Pancras Workhouse extension, which opened in March 1885 with beds for 500 old and infirm women. This extension was also by H H Bridgman, who claimed that the interior was "cheery and comfortable"; it is now the South Wing of St Pancras University Hospital.

From this corner you can either continue along Route 7, taking in Old St Pancras Church and its associated Gardens and ending with St Pancras Chambers, or seek transport home either by walking along Crowndale Road to Mornington Crescent Tube station or regaining King's Cross via Pancras Road, or Euston Road via Pancras Road and Midland Road.

Route 7
From St Pancras Gardens to St Pancras Chambers

This walk starts from the corner of Pancras Road and St Pancras Way, which can be reached by walking along Crowndale Road from the bus and Tube stops at Mornington Crescent. The walk (and this book) ends at the architectural high point of this part of the London Borough of Camden, St Pancras Chambers, which was built as the Midland Grand Hotel at the London terminus of the Midland Railway.

Walk south along **PANCRAS ROAD** towards the gardens visible to the left of the road. At a tile-hung Arts & Crafts lodge we reach **St Pancras Gardens**. A plaque on the lodge states that the gardens were completed by arrangement with the Midland Railway (MR) in 1890–91 and inaugurated on 15 July 1891. Actually, the gardens were first opened on 28 June 1877, after the Vestry had secured an Act of Parliament enabling it to take charge of St Pancras churchyard and the adjoining St Giles burial ground, and to preserve them as open spaces.

The St Giles burial ground was at this northern end of the Gardens. It was the area between the old workhouse (now St Pancras Hospital) and the Old St Pancras churchyard, and was acquired by the parish of St Giles-in-the-Fields in 1803. It then lay behind Cook's Row (p 97). Its chapel was built on the site of the Adam & Eve inn which had stood here from at least the start of 18th century. An advertisement of 1786 says the inn was "fit for the reception of the genteelest company", although in reality it was the "common resort of holiday folk" because of its trap ball ground (p 102). The tea gardens witnessed several notable ballooning events: in 1802, a Frenchman named André Garnerin made Britain's first planned parachute fall from a balloon, bailing out 10,000 feet above Bloomsbury and crash-landing at the Adam & Eve. In 1805, after the St Giles Burial Ground opened, the inn was demolished and replaced by a brick chapel, surrounded by iron gates in front of the burial ground. At the southern end of a row of houses built south of the new chapel, named Eve Terrace, a new Adam & Eve was soon built, with a remnant of the old garden laid out for bowls and flanked to the south by a terrace, called Eve Place, running at right angles to the road. After the closure of St Giles Burial Ground in 1855 its chapel was rebuilt as a National School. The former Adam & Eve and Eve Place were auctioned off in January 1878, and all these buildings had been removed by the time that St Pancras Gardens were inaugurated in 1891.

In St Giles Burial Ground were buried the sculptor John Flaxman in 1826 and the architect Sir John Soane in 1837; Soane's grave survives. Huge numbers were buried here in the 1840s – 10,000 between 1843 and 1845 alone and 3,000 in 6 months during the cholera epidemic of 1849. The stench was said to be appalling, and there were frequent complaints of body snatching and body burning to make more space. This led to a special parliamentary enquiry in 1850 to investigate 'alleged revolting practices'. A pall of smoke and smell was found to be hanging over the burial ground.

All this seems a far cry from the present St Pancras Gardens, which with the aid of a Heritage Lottery Fund grant were extensively renovated in 2000/01 and re-opened in May 2001 by the Bishop of London, assisted by the Mayor of Camden. Gates and monuments had been restored and a well-presented plan of the gardens now stands to the left of the entrance.

Ahead is the massive Burdett-Coutts memorial. Angela Burdett-Coutts was not only a millionaire philanthropist but also the Lay Rector of St Pancras and she bore the costs of this memorial which lists several dozen (once) notable people whose graves had been removed. It is surrounded by railings, and guarded by four beasts, two of whom are modelled on her own collie dog. It boasts a set of easily missed, vertically mounted sundials, a stepped pedestal and floral mosaics.

Adjoining the monument railings is an upright tombstone recalling the members of the local Purchese family (cf. Purchese Street, p 48). By the north side of the palisade, set in the ground, is a small stone recalling the composer Johann Christian Bach, the 18th child of his better-known father. Dubbed the 'English Bach', he settled in London and became musician to Queen Charlotte. Dying in debt in 1782, he was buried at St Pancras in a mass grave. He introduced the newly developed pianoforte to English audiences.

Walk round the monument and reach the iron water fountain, painted blue and surmounted by a round temple in imitation of the Temple of Vesta. It was presented by William Thornton, senior church-warden, in August 1877. Turn left along the main avenue towards the grave in the middle of the railed, circular area at the back of the grounds. This was designed by Sir John Soane (d.1837), "architect of the Bank of England". He lies buried here with his eldest son and his wife Elizabeth, who predeceased him in 1815 and for whom he erected the distinctive monument, in marble with a heavy Portland-stone canopy, which protects the tomb. Steps lead down to a vault. Its shape may be familiar because it was allegedly the inspiration for Sir Giles Gilbert Scott's design for the red K2 telephone box.

Away to the left is a small red-brick neo-Gothic building built in 1881 as the Coroner's Court. This was erected on a piece of ground consecrated by the Bishop of London in July 1866 for the reburial of the remains of closely packed decomposing bodies which had been exhumed during the MR's approach works to St Pancras station. The macabre scenes of disinterred, dismembered corpses caused a national outcry and questions in Parliament. Work was suspended, but later allowed to proceed with greater care. A further attempt by the MR in 1874 to sweep away the rest of the churchyard and the old church was firmly resisted. Overseeing the relocation of bodies, as assistant to A W Blomfield, was the young Thomas Hardy, future Wessex novelist, then living in London as a trainee architect. He later described the experience in his poem *The Levelled Churchyard*:

We late-lamented resting here,
   are mixed to human jam,
And each to each exclaims in fear,
   "I know not which I am!"

On the lawn in front of the court is a selection of gravestones. That nearest to us, by the plane tree, is to Mr William Jones (1776–1836), "for many years master of a respectable school in this parish", which a modern plaque helpfully points out was the Wellington House Academy, attended by Dickens, which was the model for Creakles's school in *David Copperfield*. Behind is a memorial to William Godwin (1756–1836) and his two wives – Mary Wollstonecraft (1759–1797), and the former Mrs Clairmont (see p 53) – who were buried in the neighbouring churchyard. Over Wollstonecraft's grave, in 1814, her daughter Mary and Percy Bysshe Shelley first confessed their undying love. The Godwins' remains were later removed to the Shelley family tomb at Bournemouth. The prominent 8-ft-high slab to the right is a memorial to John Walker (d.1807), compiler of the *Rhyming Dictionary of the English Language*, still in print.

Now walk round Soane's grave and into what was originally St Pancras churchyard (Fig 28, p 100). Ahead is the prominent "Hardy Tree", surrounded by a circular privet hedge. It has paired headstones cascading like roots from its trunk – the memorials which the future novelist rescued from destruction during the MR's works. The area behind the church was once much larger: a south-eastward extension of the graveyard occupied a field known as the Pindle, which was bought by the church in 1727. It was through this field that after its compulsory purchase the MR cut a swathe in 1866–7 to provide the approach to the new St Pancras terminus.

A little further on is a block of pink granite featuring a bar of musical notation, memorial to Samuel Webbe (1740–1816). A prolific composer of 'glees', and the first librarian of the Glee Club in 1787, he was also for 37 years organist of the Sardinian Chapel in Lincoln's Inn Fields. To the right are several, mostly illegible, table-tombs. Nearer the road is a large pink-granite memorial to numerous members of the Rhodes family, which once farmed land locally (p 63); they were prominent in parish affairs for several generations. The monument was erected in 1890 by the family's most famous son, Cecil John Rhodes (1853–1902), founder of Rhodesia (now Zambia and Zimbabwe). At the

28` St Pancras Church and Wells (drawing, c.1720)

base on the far side is a record that he was buried in the Matoppo Mountains.

Across from the Rhodes tomb by the corner of the graveyard are four gravestones standing in a row. The second, bearing a cross, is in French to Madeleine, Marquise de Tourville (1756–1837) and Antoinette Sophie de Chaumont, Vicomtesse de Buffevent (1760–1846), both émigrées. In 1791 part of the burial ground was allotted to French refugees who died in this country after the Revolution, and for whose souls masses were said in a church dedicated to St Pancras in the south of France. Bigot, last minister to Louis XVI, also lies here.

Other burials in St Pancras churchyard whose graves are no longer visible or removed included the notorious 'thief taker', Jonathan Wild, following his execution at Tyburn in 1727 (his body is said to have been subsequently disinterred and gibbeted); the architect Giacomo Leoni (d.1745), well known for his editions of Palladio and Alberti's architectural treatises; Francis Townley, executed for his part in the Jacobite rebellion of 1745; William Woollett, engraver to George III, 1783 (who has a memorial in Westminster Abbey); Pascal Paoli, the exiled Corsican patriot who died in London in 1807 (p 36); the Chevalier D'Éon, political writer and transvestite, sometime double agent of Louis XVI, who died in poverty in the guise of a woman in Millman Street

in 1810; and John Mills ("the last survivor of the Black Hole of Calcutta").

The burial ground became hopelessly overcrowded. During the 20 years up to November 1847 there were over 26,000 burials and the ground around was raised several feet by the accumulation of bodies. The problem was intensified by the cholera outbreak of 1849, and an order-in-council in 1855 discontinued burials.

Now walk back towards the Hardy Tree and round **St Pancras Old Church**, the historic heart of St Pancras.

There may possibly have been a Christian place of worship here, beside the River Fleet, since Roman times (see *Camden History Review* 21). The discovery in 1848 of a 6th-century altar-stone suggests that the church may have been rebuilt and rededicated at the time of St Augustine's mission to Britain in 597. There is a 9th-century reference to a church here, and the boundaries of the parish may have been fixed then. The building itself was first mentioned in 1183. It had major repairs from 1331 to c.1350 but then lay neglected. Norden in 1593 wrote that the church stood alone among decayed houses "without companie or comfort" and that "it is oft visited by thieves, who assembled not there to praye but to lay in wait for preye.... Walk there not too late".

In 1822 all parochial rights were transferred to the new parish church in

Euston Road. The Old Church became a chapel of ease and gradually fell into disuse. By 1847 it was derelict and virtually in ruins. As the local population grew it was decided to restore and enlarge the church. In 1847–8 it was enlarged and insensitively 'Normanised' by Alexander Gough of Gough & Roumieu, by demolishing the old square tower and using its material in extending the nave 30 feet westward and adding a squat spire on the south side. More sympathetic restorations took place in 1925, 1948 (after bomb damage) and in 1978 (by Quinlan Terry, when the parish room was created at the west end). The present, frankly ugly, church has a timber-framed and pebble-dashed belfry, and a roof of slate at the front but pantiled over the chancel. On the north side are two wall memorial plaques, one to John Horton who died aged 18 in 1735. Promising a more active future for the church was the 1996 appointment of a priest-in-charge, and the saint's day (12 May) is now celebrated by a Saint Pancras Festival.

The old church witnessed the marriage of William Godwin to Mary Wollstonecraft in 1797; that of the pantomime clown Joseph Grimaldi to his second wife in 1801; and in 1718 that of Jonathan Wild to his third. In 1760, Laurence Shirley, the 4th Earl Ferrers, famously executed for the murder of his steward, was buried under the belfry, although his remains were later removed to Staunton Harold in Leicestershire. In the church, the miniaturist Samuel Cooper, who painted Cromwell "warts and all", has an impressive wall monument showing easel and brushes, and there are busts of William Platt, 17th-century benefactor of Kentish Town, and his wife.

Walk down the steps and admire the gilded gates at the entrance to the Gardens. Then carefully cross Pancras Road and turn left along the opposite side. Look back across to the end of the churchyard, where begins a long row of brick and concrete **coal drops**, initially erected by the MR and rebuilt in the 1950s. Once the preserve of coal merchants, their cavernous brick arches are now occupied mostly by oily garages offering valeting and repairs. An exception is an up-market toy shop, formerly a ship's chandler's named Long John Silver's, where the projecting ship's figure-head, in the form of a well-endowed naked female, must bemuse, or amuse, its younger clientele. The businesses will close once the deck for the expanded St Pancras Station is built here, and a new road underneath will be constructed to link up with Goods Way.

It is hard to picture it now, but this was once the site of Pancras Wells (Fig 29), a fashionable 18th-century spa, one of several along the banks of the Fleet or 'River of Wells'. In 1700, its two pump-rooms offered a choice of purgative chalybeate water for 3d a day or half a guinea for the whole season. Stretching southwards as far as present-day Goods Way were extensive garden walks shaded by avenues of trees. By 1722 the spa's

29 Entitled the "Long Room and trap ball ground, St Pancras Wells", this puzzling southward view (1775) has the likeness of the Long Room where the Adam & Eve pub should be!

reputation had declined – there were complaints about "scandalous company" and dancing – but by 1769 the Wells had seemingly recovered its good name, its two Long Rooms advertised as able to "dine 200 compleatly". The virtues of its water in curing such diseases as King's Evil were well publicised: "it cleanses the body and sweetens the blood, and is a general and sovereign help to Nature". One print of 1729 shows various stones voided by a Mr Harrod of Hedge Row, Islington, after drinking the waters for a few days. It seems that on at least one occasion during the 18th century the Wells closed, because in 1751 a boarding school for young gentlemen on the site was being advertised. The Wells also had competition from the Adam & Eve tavern nearby; a notice of 1769 warned people that "to avoid mistakes, St Pancras Wells is on that side of the churchyard towards London".

The spa had closed by 1797, when a map shows the first houses built over its gardens. These were picturesque Church Hill, which climbed gently eastward (overlooking the churchyard). After 1800 it then continued southward as Essex Place and, eventually, Spann's Buildings (a local centre of clay pipe manufacture). Linking the latter to the main road were diminutive Dorset Place and King's Place. Facing what is now Pancras Road were Church Terrace and further south, Church Row. In 1814, Percy Bysshe Shelley, his future wife Mary and her stepsister-in-law Claire Clairmont (p 53) stayed briefly at No.5 Church Terrace after their return from Europe. Shelley was in debt, and hiding from the bailiffs. To pass the time, the party let off fireworks in the garden and dabbled in chemical experiments.

Two doors away was Baxter House, said to have been named after Richard Baxter, the 17th-century nonconformist 'divine'. From 1841 to 1862 it was occupied by the inventor (Sir) Henry Bessemer (Fig 30). In a small factory erected in the back garden he manufactured his famed 'bronze powder', an inexpensive substitute for the 'gold powder' used by japanners. An inveterate inventor, he also constructed at Baxter House a centrifugal machine for separating molasses from crystals of sugar.

Commuting from his Highgate home, he later conducted here the early experiments that led to the patenting of his celebrated 'converter', whereby steel could at last be cheaply manufactured by blowing air through molten pig-iron to remove the impurities. He had another, "secret", factory in this area, by the canal in Cambridge Street, shown as 'Besemeer's Glass Factory' on the 1851 census. Church Terrace and Church Row and the little streets behind were swept away for the building of the coal drops.

On this side of the road beyond Chenies Place (p 67) are the neo-Gothic Coal Offices of the former Purchese Street coal depot (p 46), now mainly used as workshops. Halfway along, note the brackets in the form of angels fixed on **Nos.133–135**, an antique warehouse. The furthest Coal Offices have been demolished in connection with CTRL works.

Continue towards the railway bridge and just before, branch to the right along **MIDLAND ROAD**. (Midland Road is

30   Henry Bessemer (caricature by Spy)

to be closed to traffic from spring 2003 for 2 years for the construction of a new Thameslink railway station along it and if it is also closed to pedestrians the reader may have to proceed to the St Pancras terminal by way of Brill Place and Ossulston Street.)

Cross Brill Place (p 44), with a good view of the St Pancras railway shed, a section of the ironwork still painted its original sky blue. All is red brick here and reminds one more of a Midlands scene than London. Walk on the right-hand pavement along the side of the wall, which enclosed the MR's former goods depot. When the site was cleared for this in 1878, Brewer Street (on the Brewers' estate) was renamed Midland Road, and continued roughly on the line of the former Skinner Street (on the Skinners' estate). The boundary between the two estates was near the entrance to the car park for the British Library (right).

The plot of land to our left on which St Pancras station was built was originally known as Sandhills before Sir Andrew Judd vested it in 1572 in the Skinners Company as Trustees for the benefit of Tonbridge School. It was still grassland on a map of 1785 but by the end of the 1790s the Skinners Company had begun to develop the area. First, Skinner Street (on the site of this end of Midland Road) was laid out. Along what was then the New Road, good-sized 4-storey terraced houses

– Judd Place East, and latterly Egremont Place – were built, set 50 ft back from the highway. No.13 Judd Place East was once home to the Rev. Edward Irving, the charismatic preacher and 'speaker in tongues'. When Thomas and Jane Carlyle called there to pay their respects, they were so alarmed by the "utterances" emanating from within that they made their excuses and left. Smaller streets (Skinner Place and Bedford Street) grew up behind, as far as the southern portion of the Brewers' estate, which was developed from 1811 and is now covered by the northern end of St Pancras Station.

Walk past the side of the new British Library (p 43). Opposite is the romantic skyline of **St Pancras Chambers**. Note particularly the three elongated Decorated windows which light the huge staircase within, and surmounting the highest spire an iron pennant bearing "MR" for Midland Railway. Reach **EUSTON ROAD** and turn left at the traffic lights to the former hotel entrance, embellished with stonework coats of arms and polished columns.

In 1856 a new church, St Luke's, designed by John Johnson, was started in this stretch of Euston Road (then the New Road); after delays for lack of funds, it was finally consecrated on 30 May 1861. In a 14th-century Gothic style, it had seating for 1200 people. It lasted only a few years, being taken down when St Pancras Station was built. The MR paid for the replacement church of St Luke's, Oseney Crescent, Kentish Town, designed by Basil Champneys, son of the then vicar of St Pancras. The old church was taken down and re-erected in Grove Road, Wanstead, where it opened as a congregational chapel in 1867. The local inhabitants of Somers Town got a replacement, Christ Church in Chalton Street (p 40), only through the munificence of the philanthropist George Moore.

The MR also cleared the premises at No.44 Euston Road which had housed a pioneering industrial school, called descriptively The Boy's Home for the Maintenance by their own labour of Destitute Boys Not Convicted of Crime. The school opened in a rented house here in February 1858 and was the first to be registered as an industrial school. It moved in 1865 to Regent's Park Road, Chalk Farm.

Beyond the former hotel entrance pause at the upward carriage sweep on your left to take in the full splendour of the frontage of **St Pancras Chambers**. Designed by Sir George Gilbert Scott, winner of an architectural competition, the building took eight years to complete, largely because Scott wanted high standards of finish while the MR wanted economy. Construction began in 1869 and the hotel opened to visitors on 5 May 1873, although the curved west wing was not finished until 1876. It was then known as the Midland Grand Hotel, one of the largest and finest buildings in the Gothic style in the world. This must surely be one of the most romantic scenes London has to offer. It is a delight to run one's eye over the highly decorated Gothic surface that adorns the 565-ft frontage and the 270-ft Clock Tower. Dragons – with hooked beaks, eagle's claws and crocodile tails – feature again and again. Note the addorsed dragons in the spandrels of the support for the large oriel window in the centre; underneath brackets; in some of the capitals. In the bases of the columns dividing the windows are figures supporting coats of arms, which include those of the City of London and towns (e.g. Leicester) associated with the railway.

The materials used were as far as possible from places accessible to the MR – hence among the 14 different types of stone used are Ancaster, red Mansfield and Park Spring, while slates are from Swithland and Groby quarries in Leicestershire. There are 60 million bricks and 9000 tonnes of ironwork. By March 1995 the exterior had been totally repaired at a cost of around £10 million.

The Midland Grand Hotel had over 300 bedrooms, a 100-ft dining room and a vast reading room. The latest technology was used in the design of hydraulic lifts, central heating, bathroom and kitchen planning and fire-resistant construction. An innovation in the 1890s was the ladies' smoking room, equipped with an electrophone which linked guests by telephone line to London halls and churches. Another room had a column printer that relayed Stock Exchange news and racing results.

The hotel's golden years lasted until WW I, but profits decreased thereafter. The hotel closed in 1935, when the London, Midland and Scottish Railway (LMS) took it over as offices for its Hotels Division and made crude and insensitive adaptations to the interior. LMS was subsumed into British Rail, which left in 1985 when the building failed its fire certificate, and it has been empty ever since. Famous for its grand staircase and dramatic High Victorian architecture, the building is Listed Grade I. It is popular as a film location; the Spice Girls filmed their *Wannabe* video here. Leisure group Whitbread, Marriott Hotels and the Manhattan Loft Company are working together to develop plans to return St Pancras Chambers to their original use as a luxury hotel with loft apartments on the top floors.

Walk up the ramp, under the archway and turn right into **St Pancras Station**. Before entering, note the dragon corbels to brackets so carved that water appears to be gushing out of their mouths and into the elaborately carved drainpipe heads. Now walk into the Booking Office with its linen-fold wooden panelling and many polished Purbeck marble columns. Dating from 1869, and designed by Giles Gilbert Scott, it was the most elaborate part of the station. Originally it had an open, trussed timber roof on carved hammerbeams, but this was replaced before WW II, after which the ticket office was moved to the opposite side of the hall. The corbels at the base of each arch on the wall with the clock depict a guard, a signal boy, engine driver and other railway figures carved in stone.

Proceed into the station proper for a view of the daring sweep of the train shed. Designed by W H Barlow (1812–1902), Engineer in Chief to the MR, and built 1866–8, it was and remains an engineering marvel. Wrought-iron lattice arch ribs (originally painted sky blue and all proudly bearing the legend "manufactured by the Butterley Company, Derbyshire 1867") spring from platform level and rise over 100 ft to meet in a slightly pointed apex. They cover what was then the largest enclosed space in the world. The shed is 690 ft long and 240 ft wide, and the floor acts as a tie to the arch, a daring concept that had not been attempted before. The tracks are raised 20 ft above the Euston Road so that trains could run on a level from Camden Town over the River Fleet and the Regent's Canal. The pillared vaults beneath were designed to store Burton beer barrels, a highly lucrative traffic for the MR, with a hydraulic lift to take the wagons up and down. The train shed is now much darker than when the upper part of the roof was entirely glazed with an estimated 2.5 acres of glass; most of the glass was destroyed in WW II (when the station suffered damage on several occasions) and was subsequently reduced to two narrow strips, but the drama of the great span is unimpaired. One hardly notices the electric overhead wires. John Julius Norwich wrote "in all England there is no more triumphant affirmation of the power, vitality, self-confidence and sheer panache of the Victorian age".

Major changes are likely at St Pancras Station. The train shed is to be doubled in length to handle the trains from the Continent that will run into the station once the new track from Kent through East London is laid in the next few years. Approval for this new railway was granted in 1996 by the Channel Tunnel Rail Link Act, although at the time of writing work at St Pancras Station is not scheduled for completion until 2007. On the station concourse, information boards give details of the new developments. Also here are two entrances to the Underground station.

At this high point of architectural and nostalgic emotion our book reaches its terminus.

Sources

Books and articles

Aston, Mark. *The cinemas of Camden*. LB of Camden, 1997

Barnes, Eric George. *The rise of the Midland Railway, 1844-1874*. Allen & Unwin, 1966

Barty-King, Hugh. *Maples: fine furnishers...* Quiller Press, 1992

Bebbington, Gillian. *London street names*. Batsford, 1972

Besant, Sir Walter. *London north of the Thames*. A & C Black, 1911

Brown, Stella. *A history of the London CHA Club*. The Club, 1965

Brown, W E. *Open spaces and disused burial grounds of St Pancras*. Cambridge University Press. *Bentley House and the evolution of Cambridge Publishing*. CUP, 1938

Camden History Society. *From Primrose Hill to Euston Road*. CHS, 1995

Carpenter, Kirsty. *Refugees of the French Revolution: émigrés in London 1789-1802*. Macmillan, 1999

Chambers, Colin. *The story of the Unity Theatre*. Lawrence & Wishart, 1989

Cherry, B & Pevsner, N. *London 4: North*. Penguin, 1999 (The Buildings of England)

Clarke, Linda. *Building capitalism*. Routledge, 1991 [on Somers Town]

Clinch, George, *Marylebone and St Pancras*. Truslove & Shirley, 1890

Clunn, Chris. *Eels, pie and mash*. Museum of London, 1995

Cumming, E & Kaplan, W. *The Arts & Crafts movement*. Thames & Hudson, 1991

Denford, Steven L J. *Agar Town: the life & death of a Victorian 'slum'*. CHS, 1995

Denyer, C H (ed.). *St Pancras through the centuries*. Le Play House Press, 1935

Essex Lopresti, M. *Exploring the Regent's Canal*. Brewin, 1987

Evinson, Denis. *Catholic churches of London*. Sheffield Academic Press, 1998

Fairfield, S. *The streets of London: a dictionary ...* Macmillan, 1983

Fellows, Richard. *Edwardian architecture: style & technology*. Lund Humphries, 1995

Fletcher, Geoffrey. *London at my feet*. Daily Telegraph, 1980

Forster, John. *Life of Charles Dickens*. New ed. Dent, 1966

Foster, D. *Alehouses [etc]* (at Westminster Archives)

Gilbert, Bob. *The King's Cross Cut...King's Cross Canal Project*, 1985

Gough, Janine. *20 years of 'planning' the Tolmers Square development*. Middlesex Polytechnic, 1981

Graves, Algernon. *The Royal Academy of Arts: a complete dictionary of contributors ... 1769-1904*. Henry Graves, 1905-6

Greater London Council. *Historic buildings in London: an inventory of buildings owned by the [GLC]*. Academy Editions, 1975

Highmore, Anthony. *Pietas Londinensis: ...public charities in and near London*. 1810

Holmes, Malcolm J. *Housing is not enough*. St Pancras Housing Assoc., 1999

Holmes, Malcolm J. (comp.) *Somers Town: a record of change*. LB of Camden, 1985

Howkins, C D. "Somers Town between the Wars", in *Camden Journal*, Dec.1971

Hunter, M & Thorne, R (eds). *Change at King's Cross*. Historical Publications, 1990

Irvine, L & Atterbury, P. *Gilbert Bayes, sculptor, 1872-1953*. Richard Dennis, 1998

Jones, Gareth S. *Outcast London*. Clarendon Press, 1971

Joseph, Adam. *King of the Pearly Kings: the story of Henry Croft*. Cockney Museum, 1975

Le Faye, Deirdre. *Medieval Camden*. CHS, 1975

Lee, Charles E. *St Pancras Church and Parish*. St Pancras Church, 1955

London County Council. *Survey of London*, vol.19 (1938), vol.21 (1949), vol.24 (1952)

Manton, Jo. *Elizabeth Garrett Anderson*. Methuen, 1965

Maple & Co. *The house of Maple*. [The company], 1964

Mee, Arthur. *London*. Hodder & S, 1937 (The King's England)

Miller, Frederick. *St Pancras past and present*. Abel Heywood, 1874

Morrell, Rev. Conyers. *The story of Agar Town: the ecclesiastical parish of St Thomas...* Premo Press, 1935

Napley, Sir David. *The Camden Town murder*. Weidenfeld, 1987

Newton, Douglas. *Catholic London*. Hale, 1950

Oakley, E R. *The London County Council Tramways, vol 2: North London*. London Tramways History Group, 1991

Olsen, Donald J. *The growth of Victorian London*. Batsford, 1976

Olsen, Donald J. *Town planning in London: the 18th and 19th centuries*. Yale UP, 1964

Palmer, Samuel. *St Pancras…* [The author], 1870

Pevsner, Nikolaus. *London, except the Cities of London and Westminster*. Penguin, 1952 (The Buildings of England)

Renton Howard Wood Partnership. *Tolmers Square development report…*, 1973-74

Richardson, Joanna. *Baudelaire*. Murray, 1994

Richardson, John. *Camden Town and Primrose Hill past.* Historical Publications, 1991

Richardson, John. *A history of Camden*. Historical Publications, 1999

Robertson, Brian. *Roman Camden*. CHS, 1977

Saint, Andrew (ed.). *Politics and the people of London: the LCC 1889-1965*. Hambledon P, 1989

St Clair, William. *The Godwins and the Shelleys*. Faber, 1989

St Pancras (Met. Borough). *The end of one story: a souvenir of the Borough…1965 [St Pancras House of Fellowship]*. 1943 (untitled pamphlet)

Scholey, K A *The railways of Camden*. CHS, 2002

Service, Alastair. *Edwardian architecture*. Thames & Hudson, 1977

Simmons, Jack. *St Pancras Station*. Allen & Unwin, 1968

Sinclair, Frederick (comp.) *St Pancras through the ages*. MB of St Pancras, 1938

Smithson, Alison & Peter. *The Euston Arch and the growth of the [LMS] Railway*. Thames & Hudson, 1968

Stewart, C J. *The housing question in London*. LCC, 1900

Tindall, Gillian. *The fields beneath.* Temple Smith, 1977

Tolmers Village Action Group. *The Tolmers people plan*. [1977?]

Uwins, Sarah. *A memoir of Thomas Uwins RA*. 1859, reprinted EP Publishing, 1978

Wainwright, David. *The piano makers*. Hutchinson, 1975

Walford, Edward. *Old and new London*, 1872; reprinted as *London recollected*, Alderman Press, 1987

Waterhouse, Paul. "The Euston Road", in *Architectural Review*, Town Planning & Housing Suppl, December 1910, pp 303-7

Wates, Nick. *The battle for Tolmers Square*. Routledge, 1976

Weinreb, B & Hibbert, C (eds) *The London encyclopaedia*. Macmillan, 1992

Whitley, W T. *The Baptists of London, 1612–1928*. Kingsgate Press, 1928

Whytehead, R & Blackmore, L. "Excavations at Tottenham Court, 250 Euston Road", in *LAMAS Transactions*, vol.34 (1983)

Wilson, Colin St John. *The design & construction of the British Library*. BL, 1998

Yalom, Marilyn. *Blood sisters: the French Revolution in women's memory*. Pandora, 1995

Maps

Rocque 1746
Horwood 1799
Thompson 1801/1804 (& terrier book)
Davies 1834
Greenwood 1834
Britton 1834
parish 1849 & 1861
Stanford 1862
Cassell 1862
Ordnance Survey 1871 & later
Bacon 1888
Booth's poverty maps 1889–98
Goad insurance maps
LCC bomb damage maps.

Other sources

Chambers biographical dictionary
Dictionary of national biography
Who was who

Camden (London Borough), Dept of Planning and Communications: agendas & reports
Census, 1841–1891
LCC/GLC street lists
London County Council: Education Committee minutes
London County Council: Housing Committee minutes
Post Office/Kelly's London directories
St Pancras (Met. Borough): Housing Committee minutes
St Pancras Vestry: rate books
School Board for London: annual reports

Camden Citizen
Camden Journal
Camden New Journal
St Pancras Journal

Camden History Review (as noted in text)
Camden History Society. *Newsletters*

www.camden.gov.uk/ planning [for Listed buildings]
www.knowuk.co.uk

Camden Local Studies and Archives Centre (including Ambrose Heal Collection)
Guildhall Library
London Metropolitan Archives
National Monuments Record (English Heritage)

110